"*Finding Home* offers luminous, grounded wisdom from a luminous, grounded writer. Julie Aageson invites us into a journey of spiritual reflection upon the things that matter most—relationship, story, divine indwelling, vocation, generosity, gratitude, failure, and those pesky questions of meaning underlying them all. Read with pen in hand, this book will open the reader to undiscovered corners of their own soul."

—**Laurie Larson Caesar**
Bishop, Oregon Synod, Evangelical Lutheran Church in America

"In this world we have no abiding city, and yet here is Julie Aageson conjuring that world in the olive groves of Palestine, the smoky fires of wintry England, the saltwater flats of her childhood. Attention must be paid to its haunting beauty and instability—to the loving but desperate asylum seeker, to the kindly parent unmoored by depression—for in it we find the suffering and redeeming God, our heart's true home."

—**William Craft**
President, Concordia College, Moorhead, Minnesota

"To be human is to be a homemaker! If you thought you had risen above all that, Aageson shows us how we all want and need to make of every one of our human experiences a place to hunker down, body and soul, and take root. We long to be at home and whole. As we spiral through our developmental cycles and find ourselves off center and clumsily groping, it is some solid sense of arriving at home we grapple for. More than an actual roof, we finally want to be at home in ourselves . . . we want the Divine to find a home in us."

—**Gertrud Mueller Nelson**
Liturgical artist and author of *Here All Dwell Free*

"Wanderers, wonderers, seekers, and centered ones—come on in! Julie Aageson's *Finding Home* is a safe place where you can let down your defenses and, with unguarded hearts and utter gratitude, rest in her rich hospitality."

—**Mike Woods**
Pastor, Prince of Peace Lutheran Church

FINDING HOME

Prior Publications by Julie K. Aageson

One Hope: Re-Membering the Body of Christ (Augsburg Fortress and Liturgical Press, 2015) (Co-authored in commemoration of the 500th anniversary of the Protestant Reformation)

Benedictions: 26 Reflections (Wipf and Stock, 2016)

Holy Ground: An Alphabet of Prayer (Cascade Books, 2018)

Finding Home

Julie K. Aageson

CASCADE *Books* · Eugene, Oregon

FINDING HOME

Cascade Books
An Imprint of Wipf and Stock Publishers
199 W. 8th Ave., Suite 3
Eugene, OR 97401

www.wipfandstock.com

PAPERBACK ISBN: 978-1-7252-7602-4
HARDCOVER ISBN: 978-1-7252-7603-1
EBOOK ISBN: 978-1-7252-7604-8

Cataloguing-in-Publication data:

Names: Aageson, Julie K., author.

Title: Finding home / Julie K. Aageson.

Description: Eugene, OR: Cascade Books, 2020 | Includes bibliographical
references.

Identifiers: ISBN 978-1-7252-7602-4 (paperback) | ISBN 978-1-7252-7603-1
(hardcover) | ISBN 978-1-7252-7604-8 (ebook)

Subjects: LCSH: Home | Spirituality | Spiritual life—Christianity

Classification: BV4501 A132 2020 (print) | BV4501 (ebook)

Manufactured in the U.S.A.   JULY 15, 2020

For my beloved grandchildren: Ingrid and Elliot, Elsa and Holden, Kai and Kieran, the "littles" who grace our home with joy and gladness. May each of you know the deep pleasure of finding home. May you learn to be at home with yourselves, knowing both rootedness and the security of belonging. May you discover home away from home and what it means to be at home in many places. Most of all, may you see the world and yourselves through the eyes and heart of the Holy One, finding home where God dwells.

Contents

Permissions

"A Story of Adoption," pp. 2–3. Use of the poem, "Who Am I?" From *Letters and Papers from Prison: Revised, Enlarged Edition* by Dietrich Bonhoeffer, translated from the German by R. H. Fuller, Frank Clark, et al. Copyright 1953, 1967, 1971 by SCM Press Ltd. Reprinted with the permission of Scribner, a division of Simon and Schuster, Inc. All rights reserved

"No Crib for a Bed," p. 62. Use of the poem "Christ the Door" by Samuel Torvend, Senior historian, Department of Religion at Pacific Lutheran University, Tacoma, Washington.

"Questions of Faith," p. 73. Copyright 2004 by the *Christian Century*, "If God is Your Answer" by Warren L. Molton is reprinted by permission from the June 15, 2004, issue of the *Christian Century*.

Introduction

So many images swim just below the surface of my memory, all the houses where I came to know home. It takes little to retrieve them: a shared story told for decades in the varied iterations of the various tellers; smells like the acrid pungency of saltwater tide flats on the island where I grew up or of wafting smoke from coal fires on a drizzly winter day in England; the sound of rain on a tin roof or the whishing gasps of a braking bus. Sure triggers are memories of births and birthdays, of holy days and holidays, of arrivals and departures—flashing through one's mind like a slow-motion movie filled with familiar faces and poignant reminders of time and place, houses and home.

They came in all shapes and sizes: a tiny box of home set in a small mountain town; a narrow house made of corrugated steel and named "the tin house" by my young sisters and me; my grandparents' homes, the one built on an outcrop of rock overlooking the channel where ships and ferries crisscrossed day after day and the other, a large, white-sided arts and crafts home surrounded by fruit trees and well-tended gardens. This one appears often in my dreams and became the family gathering place with its seemingly endless spaces for hiding and playing and discovering family stories.

There are apartments and flats where we learned to live in close proximity with others, an island cabin made of hand-hewn logs and a mountain house near a river, both of these iconic in their larger-than-life roles. In Minnesota, we found our dream house during my daughters' growing up years—an elegant old English Tudor where we hosted sleep-overs and faculty gatherings and students from around the world.

Home, of course, is so much more than houses. Knowing ourselves to be made in the image of God is one place to begin. In our lifelong endeavor to know and be known by God—to see the world and ourselves through the eyes and heart of the Holy One—is to know grace, the very essence of the love we believe God to be. As children we begin with the wonder of birth, the story of the Nativity and multilayered meanings of incarnation, God taking human form and coming to us in the Christ child, Jesus. And if we are fortunate enough to move beyond literal images and interpretations, we begin to think about the spirit of God living within each of us, both immanent and transcendent. Then we catch glimpses of God within as well as without, a way of seeing the universe as God's body and ourselves as the body of Christ.

Knowing ourselves to be made in the likeness of God is another kind of home, another of the graces of God's boundless and unutterable love. As recipients of and receptacles for God's love and very form, we too are Christ-bearers. We too are called to be love and mercy and grace for a hurting world. We are God's home. We have been made in the image of God and charged with sharing the infinite love of the Holy One shown to us in the world we call home. The very face of God is revealed everywhere we look, a God who makes the ordinary holy, the mundane sacred. "Cleave the wood and I am there," says the writer in the apocryphal gospel of Thomas. "Lift up the stone, and you will find me there." And in becoming God's home, we know ourselves to be truly home. This new way of being is pure grace, another of the ways we discern the immeasurable love of God.

For me, creating and making a home is primal, instinctual, spiritual. Home in all its iterations—literal and metaphorical—defines our identity. Perhaps this is universal. For all fortunate enough to know the security of home, the act of recalling those places where we first knew ourselves to belong sometimes elicits complex and complicated feelings.

When my children were growing up, we often talked with them about how important it is to be "at home" in many different places. In part, we wanted them to be able to adapt and adjust to the moves and travel of their childhood. It was also our way of helping them know the importance of rootedness. But perhaps more than either of these was our desire for them to be at home with themselves, at home in the world, and able to say, "We were at home there."

Finding Home is a collection of reflections about some multifaceted meanings of home. What does it mean to "be home" for others—a safe place, a place of grace? What does it mean to "be home" ourselves, for ourselves? Can we see the face of the Holy One in the weary desperation of refugees or in a homeless woman and her children as they struggle to survive? When we sometimes comment about a person who seems confident as "being at home in her own skin," what does that mean? What, exactly, *is* home?

Uoc and Bay were refugees. They arrived in the fall of the year, still shell-shocked by their tortuous journey from an obscure Vietnamese village where news of the outside world, let alone the United States, was practically non-existent. Uoc and Bay were the older couple—in their early twenties. They came with two small children and with Bay's younger sister and her husband. None of them spoke any English. None of them were literate in their own language. They were simply, and not so simply, trying to survive. Through all the losses, all the chaos, their painful search was for safety, security, shelter. Now nearly forty years later, I still feel their longing.

Linda was adopted as an infant. Her devoted parents showered her with a secure home, the riches of family life, unconditional love. Now in her seventies and with a growing family of her own, she longed to know more about her birth mother and father, possible siblings, the people with whom she shared genetic similarities. She wanted the wholeness of knowing herself more fully in order to understand some of her own characteristics, talents, interests—a way of coming home to herself.

Introduction

For many years my spouse and I took turns making and sharing meals at a local homeless shelter. One Christmas when our daughters were still at home, we all celebrated Christmas Day dinner with the residents at the shelter. Their palpable fragility and vulnerability exposed our own uneasiness, our own awareness of privilege, our own avoidance of brokenness. And yet there was a tangible sense of home in that shelter for people without a home.

What is it like to be a refugee fleeing unimaginable suffering and loss of identity? How much desperation, how much fear does it take to leave the only home you know, a home you know you will never see again? When every door has closed, when daily life is unbearable, when one's very identity is shattered, what is home like? What, exactly, *is* home?

Home and all its meanings always is characterized by joy and sorrow, grief and gladness, complex combinations of the realities of complicated lives. As you consider the places where you find home, may you *be* home not only for yourself but also for others, making space for compassion and kindness, familiarity and difference, shelter and security, places where God dwells.

Finding home is a radical act of claiming a place in the world. In these reflections, may you discover new ways for thinking about the countless meanings of home: what it means to be at home in many places, the importance of rootedness, what it is to be homeless or a refugee fleeing for a new life. Perhaps you will recall physical homes where you learned who you are and who God is. But more than these things, may you know yourself to be made in the image of God—imago Dei, at home with yourself, comfortable in your own skin, and at home in a fascinatingly diverse world. We *are* God's dwelling place. We *are* God's home and the whole world is the house of God. Finding home indeed!

1

A STORY OF ADOPTION

HE SAT AT MY table surrounded by friends before taking a long and deep breath. "I don't want to dominate the conversation," she said, "but there are some things I'd like to share with you and it's a long story." Her quiet tentativeness and somber voice signaled something important and we all assured her that we did indeed want to hear what she wanted to tell. So with the rapt attention of everyone around that table, Linda began to describe the story of her identity.

She was adopted as an infant. Her devoted parents showered her with a secure home, the riches of family life, unconditional love. Now in her seventies and with a growing family of her own, she longed to know more about her birth mother and father, possible siblings, the people with whom she shared genetic similarities. She wanted the wholeness of knowing herself more fully in order to understand some of her own characteristics, talents, interests— a way of coming home to herself. And so Linda made the decision to take a DNA test, a brave move to discover possible ancestry, perhaps even the identity of her birth family. Now she waited.

Sometime later, Linda received the results of her test together with subsequent contacts for people who shared DNA so similar to hers that the likelihood of their being related was pretty much conclusive. Soon after, she was contacted by one of these "relatives," a newly discovered sister with whom Linda shared her birth father and three brothers. What Linda wanted to describe to us that summer day around our table was her hopeful apprehension about discovering her birth relatives, the pieces of her home, the identity she'd never known.

All of us wrestle with questions of identity. Perhaps the recent popularity of DNA testing confirms a universal longing to know more fully who we are. Knowing our stories, even our genetic makeup, helps us know ourselves. When I was still a teenager, my father gave me a copy of Dietrich Bonhoeffer's moving poem, "Who Am I?" written from the confines of a Nazi prison cell shortly before his death. Bonhoeffer's poignant words have accompanied me throughout my life . . .

Who am I? They often tell me
I stepped from my cell's confinement
Calmly, cheerfully, firmly,
Like a squire from his country house.

Who am I? They often tell me
I used to speak to my warders
Freely and friendly and clearly,
As though it were mine to command.

Who am I? They also tell me
I bore the days of misfortune
Equably, smilingly, proudly,
like one accustomed to win.

Am I then really all that which others tell of?

Or am I only what I myself know of myself?
Restless and longing and sick, like a bird in a cage,
Struggling for breath, as though hands were compressing my throat,
Yearning for colors, for flowers, for the voices of birds,
Thirsting for words of kindness, for neighborliness,
Tossing in expectation of great events,

A Story of Adoption

Powerlessly trembling for friends at an infinite distance,
Weary and empty at praying, at thinking, at making,
Faint, and ready to say farewell to it all?

Who am I? This or the other?
Am I one person today and tomorrow another?
Am I both at once? A hypocrite before others,
And before myself a contemptibly woebegone weakling?
Or is something within me still like a beaten army
Fleeing in disorder from victory already achieved?

Who am I? They mock me, these lonely questions of mine.
Whoever I am, Thou knowest, O God, I am thine![1]

Bonhoeffer was struggling to make sense of his life, grappling to find meaning in the chaos of a madman's takeover of his beloved country. He knew that death likely awaited him.

The insecurities and self-doubts that plague us all can rob us of being at home with ourselves. Sometimes we struggle with who we are. We may not have had the experience of actual adoption or discovering a birth family later in life. But most of us know the life-long vagaries of finding our identity and liking our own company.

The truth is that we are, all of us, adopted sons and daughters. We long to belong, to be loved, to find home within ourselves. The apostle Paul reminds us in his New Testament letters that we are adopted by God, made heirs, given the right to be named by God and to inherit God's identity. With Bonhoeffer, we can say with confidence, "Whoever I am, Thou knowest, O God, I am thine!"

Linda's meetings with her birth siblings helped her make sense of a family legacy of music, of educated parents whose life circumstances made it impossible to marry and care for a child, of beloved adoptive parents. She was able to incorporate that missing part of her identity into an already satisfyingly full life and in so doing, she discovered a sense of wholeness and a coming home to herself. When, as a twelve year old, Linda heard for the first time the adoption texts in Paul's letters, she knew herself to be home

---

1. Dietrich Bonhoeffer, *Letters and Papers from Prison* (New York: Macmillan, 1971), 347–48.

for good. As adopted sons and daughters, we are, all of us, home. *Whoever I am, thou knowest, O God, I am thine.*

REFLECTION

All of us wrestle with questions of identity. Knowing our stories helps us know ourselves. "Who am I?" wrote Dietrich Bonhoeffer from the confines of his prison cell . . .

- Name some ways life circumstances, self-doubt, and insecurities rob us of being at home with ourselves.

- How do you understand Bonhoeffer's words or the apostle Paul's description of being adopted daughters and sons of God?

- How might Linda's experience of adoption and longing to know her history resonate for all of us as we wrestle with feeling at home with who we are? Of knowing ourselves to be home? Of liking our own company?

2

ALONG THE
HEBRON ROAD

HE MEWLING CRIES OF feral cats nesting on our window ledges made it hard to sleep at night. In the heat of summer, we were grateful for the iron bars that kept the cats out while allowing cooler night air inside. When daylight came and we could walk the rocky grounds of the Tantur Ecumenical Institute along the Hebron Road on our way into Bethlehem, those same skittish cats roamed the brown, barren hills in search of something to fill their empty stomachs. In search of food ourselves, we were on our way to Awad's, a Palestinian green grocer and the easiest place to find fresh food in spite of the thorny walk through the old olive groves of Tantur.

It was the summer of 2000 and again the peace talks between President Bill Clinton, Yasser Arafat, and Ehud Barak had fallen apart. Riding into Jerusalem along the Hebron Road and back again in the evening, the tension among the mostly Palestinian Arab passengers in our local cheroot hung heavy as they debated the failure of the peace talks and lamented their own losses. It wasn't our first exposure to the Israeli-Palestinian conflict and we'd experience several more tense visits in coming years.

That same Hebron Road used to be the route of choice between Jerusalem and Bethlehem. Before the Israeli wall was built, a major checkpoint marked the border between the two cities. Now part of the barrier wall separating the West Bank from Israel, Israelis keep careful watch on who comes and who goes along the Hebron Road. For our friends, a Palestinian family with roots that go back centuries in Bethlehem as well as family origins in Jerusalem, finding home is nearly impossible. For all their adult lives Micheal and Carmen have tried to make home in both places, mostly with agonizing difficulty. Family members live both in the West Bank and in Jerusalem, never quite sure just where home is. Their story is common.

In the 1940s along the Hebron Road, a Zionist youth movement helped resettle Kfar Etzion, an abandoned kibbutz in a place densely populated by Arabs. It was the third return of the Jews to the area within the borders of the newly proposed Arab state and it became a classic example of Jews and Arabs at war over finding a home. The thousands of Arabs who'd lived there for centuries finally were defeated and today the nearby hills along the Hebron Road are inhabited by Israelis, also claiming their right of return. Revenge, hatred, and fury over the lands along the Hebron Road continue to rage.

What is a home? Most would agree it's a place whose walls and borders are protected and honored, a safe place where shelter and daily life is stable, constant, peaceful. But for Israelis and Palestinians no such home exists. Israel was established so that Jewish people, who have rarely felt at home in the world, finally would have a home. But after more than seventy years, Israel still is not a stable, peaceful home for Jews. And for Palestinians who understand the same land to have been their home for centuries, who call the Israelis "occupiers," and who have been brutally oppressed decade after decade, home has become an unrelenting nightmare. In many ways, the fortress that is Israel and the subjugation that is Palestine is in a sense not home for either.

In 1948 when Dalia's Jewish family immigrated to Israel from Bulgaria with 50,000 other Jews, they moved into a large and beautiful home in the old Palestinian city of Ramle. Dalia grew up in that beautiful house always aware that something was not quite right. While she didn't remember the day they moved into "their" new house—a pot of warm soup still on the stove, lemons hanging from lush trees in the garden, clothing and furniture scattered around the house—she knew somehow that it wasn't really "her" home. Years later when Dalia was a university student home on break, three well-dressed young Palestinian men came to see the house. It was Dalia's first encounter with Palestinians and she knew instinctively that she and they had much to talk about.

That day began a friendship between Bashir, the son whose Muslim father had built this beautiful house and who had been forced to leave it at age six, and Dalia, the daughter of Jewish refugees seeking a new home in Israel. Despite chasm-wide differences in political views, Dalia and Bashir and their families have struggled to share their common humanity and mutual desire to live together in harmony. Today at Bashir's request and with Dalia's support, their house serves as an open house—a home—for Arab and Jewish children, a center of reconciliation focused on the needs of children. The director of Dalia's and Bashir's "Open House" is a Palestinian Christian, thus completing the circle representing the three great religions all claiming home in this conflicted land.

Along the Hebron Road and across the conflicted Middle East, everyone longs for home, a place to live in freedom and peace and safety, where lives are free from subjugation and enslavement. Most are looking for basic humanity, for dignity and respect, for release from the fanatic interests and global interference that continue to fuel division and hatred. It's an old story of tortured anguish and suffering.

In this land where Jews, Christians, and Muslims share both common ancestry and historical animosities, there are few signs of hope and reconciliation. It's a painfully enlarged microcosm of what happens when humankind cannot tolerate difference and differing points of view. The haunting cries of the feral cats outside our windows at Tantur somehow evoke the grief and sorrow of this land. Finding a common home for Palestinians and Israelis will have to be mutual. One will not find home if the other has no home.

REFLECTION

Along the Hebron Road and across the conflicted Middle East, everyone longs for home, a place to live in freedom and peace and safety where lives are free from subjugation and enslavement.

- Do you agree that the fortress that is Israel and the subjugation that is Palestine is not a home for either? Why or why not?

- How might the work of people like Bashir and Dalia slowly change the future for Israelis and Palestinians?

- Talk about some other places around the world in similar conflicts. How might they differ and what do they have in common with Israelis and Palestinians?

3

AN ORDERED HOUSE IN A DISORDERED WORLD

Waking up this morning, I smile. Twenty-four brand new hours are before me. I vow to live fully in each moment and to look at all beings with eyes of compassion.[1]

 aspire to these wise words from Buddhist monk Thich Nhat Hanh. But as each day gets crazier and the threats and actions darker and more sinister, a smile at waking each morning is sometimes challenging. Our nation has endured an extraordinary season of frightening political crises the effects of which continue to ricochet around the world.[2] This isn't unique to our country of course and crises of one kind or another seem to be our common lot. Nevertheless, the disorder of the

---

1. Thich Nhat Hanh, *Gathas of Thich Nhat Hanh*. Online at https://beherenownetwork.com/thich-nhat-hanh-gathas.

2. The tenure of Donald Trump as president of the United States that began in 2016 was fraught with crises including dishonesty, impeachment, abuse of presidential power, a global pandemic, and inflamed racial tensions.

world seems especially relevant as I write today. Perhaps a little amnesia would not be so bad.

So before the day begins and while my eyes still are closed, I begin to plan: a gathering for family, a summer project, the day that lies ahead. I vow to live fully in each moment and I hope to have the grace to see all beings with eyes of compassion, doing my best to squeeze in those who cause so much of the chaos and fear. Notes are written, prayers are offered, I make my bed. Primroses wait to be planted in the pots that line the garden. Soup and bread need to be made. The business of finding a home in the world goes on.

Marie Kondo, the Japanese guru who advises us to tidy our homes, get rid of clutter, of things that do not "spark joy," is hovering over the ether of disorder and inviting our best intentions. "Get rid of all this stuff," she says. "What are you waiting for? Simplify your life." The ubiquitous presence of storage units that seem to sprout like mushrooms in every American city point to a culture consumed with too much stuff and Kondo knows her audience. Perhaps storage units are an homage to our longing for order, for living fully in each moment? Might there be containers where we could lock away the disorder that keeps us awake at night—storage units for liquidating political crises, dreaded medical diagnoses, the unexpected death of a spouse? I need order in a disordered world.

Perhaps it's a characteristic of first-borns but I confess to having always been a neat-nik. Siblings, colleagues, and my own children can attest to my need for order. To my mind the beauty and symmetry of order are freeing. I understand the dark side, the need to impose control or avoid spontaneity and the serendipitous. And there will be no debate from me about the benefits of being "laid back," a state of being my daughters used to wish their parents exhibited more often. But I want order in my house, the rooms that make up daily life, the body that houses my soul, my spirit, the places I call home.

Pablo Picasso's painting called *The Three Musicians* helped inspire a children's book of the same title. It's a story about a beast that traumatizes a kingdom with fear and foreboding and lies. There is no joy, no laughter, no trust. Anxious eyes filled with distress peer out from every window. Into this barren village kingdom paralyzed by fright and disorder come Picasso's three brightly clothed musicians playing their instruments and dancing . . . perhaps you can imagine the rest of the story.

We can be the three musicians who help bring order (joy, laughter, peace, trust) to our own homes, our own villages, our nation. We can help carry one another, rebuilding what has been lost, helping restore dignity and integrity and an ordered house. We can make music and dance, helping one another cope with fear, listening and responding in love, showing hospitality and welcome, using our voices to speak truth, even with protests and vigilant dissent. In this disordered world, finding joy and peace in the order of our homes and our spirits is no small feat. With Thich Nhat Hanh, vow to live fully in each moment, plant a garden, make music, write a letter, bake bread, share a pot of soup, visit a neighbor, plan a new project, make a list of "must-read" books, restore order to *your* home, one room at a time.

Home is a basic existential experience. It can be the literal house where we live, a geographical setting, the people with whom we feel most at home and the places where that happens, our physical and psychological states, the work we do, the things that bring peace to our souls and our spirits—all are factors for defining existence and the meaning of home. Each helps describe who we are and where we find home. Each shapes how we live and how we cope.

So when the day is over and I close my eyes to sleep, I want my house to be in order. I want to lay down my head in peace and in gratitude, mindful of the day nearly over, of things done and left undone, letting them be. I want to put away my fears of the darkness of the world and look with hope and with courage to a new day ahead. I know I am not alone. And when the disordered world claws its way back into consciousness and I find myself tethered again to an ever-expanding panoply of worries, I will look for you, my companions along the way, for direction and peace. We all prefer an ordered house.

REFLECTION

So when the day is over and I close my eyes to sleep, I want my house to be in order.

- What are some of the beasts that traumatize "your kingdom"?
- Do you resonate to the deeper meanings of order? Why or why not?
- How do you make order in your house?
- How do you keep order in your home?

4

At home
in our bodies

HAT DOES IT MEAN to be at home in one's body? Truth to tell, most of us struggle at one time or another with being at home in our own skin, content with who we are, comfortably pleased with the bodies that house our spirits, our souls. Sometimes our bodies let us down. Having trusted and perhaps taken physical well-being for granted, suddenly a frightening diagnosis reminds us that we too are vulnerable, our bodies unpredictable, good health not a guarantee. It may even feel as if our body has betrayed us. Sometimes our bodies make us uncomfortable.

So much can go wrong. It seems to me that nearly every day I read yet another warning describing "ten signs" that might indicate heart disease, Alzheimer's, diabetes, Parkinson's, or any number of dreaded cancers. Take your pick—the list of maladies that seem to lurk and prey is endless. Today's warning on my newsfeed was for pancreatic cancer and the first sign was lower back pain. Limping along after having twisted my own back recently, my mind immediately is off and running: "what if? could it be? pay attention!"

This week a stem cell transplant begins for the five-year-old son of long-time friends. His leukemia diagnosis several months ago has been a roller-coaster ride of treatments, hoped for remission, dashed hopes, and desperation. Now his parents have had to make a decision no one should have to consider: harvesting healthy cells from their three-year-old son to save the life of his big brother. Bodies! So much can go wrong.

Growing up female in the fifties and sixties (and thirties, forties, and ad infinitum), many of us wrestled with learning to accept and love our bodies. It didn't help that biblical texts sometimes set the body against the spirit or that a Puritan ethic often associated the body with sin and was suspicious of physical pleasure. Some wildly misguided idea that a "perfect body" was a possibility if one exercised enough or used this product or lost or gained so many pounds or wore one's hair in a certain style plagued too many of us. Our culture makes an art of bizarre notions of physical perfection. And of course comfort with our bodies is not a challenge limited to women or to growing up in a certain time period. Why is it too often difficult to be at home in our own skin?

Knowing that we are mortal beings, feeling truly at home in our physical bodies may not be possible. But for now, can we love the body that houses our spirit? Can we celebrate the distinctive bodily characteristics that make each of us unique, one of a kind, "me"? Can we recognize the beauty of physical pleasure and embrace *without reservation* the body we've been given?

Bodies do matter a lot in the Christian tradition. We believe ourselves to be part of the body of Christ, the church. We know the importance of incarnation, the mystery of God taking human form to be born among us in the body of Jesus. The Eucharist is a bodily meal—bread and wine, body and blood—given for the life of the world. I do not begin to understand the many meanings of these holy things. But I do know that my body and yours together with the bodies of those who are hungry and sick and orphaned and maimed matter to God. I do know that we, all of us, are made in God's image. I do know that being made in the likeness of the

Holy One means that I can find home in my body and in the bodies of others.

This amazing claim ought to give us pause and waken in us profound gratitude not only for our physical bodies—hearts that continue to pump life-giving blood, lungs that filter the air we breathe, arms and legs, fingers and toes, eyes and ears. But deep gratitude too for the spirit that enlivens us and the ways our minds and spirits help us see that same mind and spirit in the flesh-and-blood bodies of others, especially those who seem different from us.

Within this flesh-and-blood home that is our bodily frame, the spirit of God dwells. The Holy One inhabits and animates us with the very breath of life that began at our birth. Our bodies are dwelling places, homes. If the divine spirit finds home within us, surely we too can be at home in the bodies that house our spirits, our souls, and the spirit of God.

REFLECTION

Bodies matter a lot in the Christian tradition. But what does it mean to be at home with oneself, at home with one's flesh-and-blood body? Truth to tell, most of us struggle at one time or another with being at home in our own skin, content with who we are, comfortably pleased with the bodies that house our spirits, our souls.

- Knowing that we are mortal beings, feeling truly at home in our physical bodies may not be possible. But for now, can we love the body that houses our spirit?

- How might a Christian emphasis on the importance of the body help us rethink the ways we are at home in our own skin?

- How might biblical texts that set body against spirit or the Puritan suspicion of the body influence our attitudes about being at home in our bodies?

- How might our acceptance of ourselves, of our bodies, impact the ways we view and accept others?

- What does it mean to you to make peace with your body?

- What are some implications for being made in the image of God, Imago Dei?

5

BANBURY ROAD

 E ARRIVED BY TRAIN early in the fall of the year. Michaelmas Term would begin in October and we needed time to get our bearings, learn the lay of the land, and make a new home. From the train station where we were met by a friend that early September afternoon, we made our way through the maze of narrow roads that encircle so many of the Oxford colleges—ribbon-like lanes meandering in every direction and finally connecting to Banbury Road, a busy thoroughfare that would lead us to our new English home.

We were weary from a long season of farewells, from moving and packing and storing most of our earthly possessions. After one last send-off from family and a long, trans-Atlantic trek, that first trip up Banbury Road was as emotional for us as for our young daughters. We had no idea how long this graduate school venture would take. We did not know how English life would suit our small family, how we'd adjust to living cheek to jowl with other uprooted families from around the world, whether the work that brought us would come to fruition, or what the economic and psychological realities would look like.

What we did know was that Banbury Road led to our new home, an imposingly ugly four-story complex of cinder-block flats where we hoped we'd settle into a challenging new life. We did not expect to find home in so inauspicious a space. But of course the larger place was anything but inauspicious and that tiny flat and the tears it initially evoked became as richly auspicious as the unforgettable spires, the people we'd meet, and the extraordinary experiences we would share.

Do not judge a book by its cover, the well-worn adage goes. And indeed, the flat into which we moved was not a beauty. But what happened there and in the peculiar traditions and ancient surroundings of an old British university town over the course of the next years would mark our lives forever.

Home is shaped dramatically by the people who inhabit our lives. From the beginning, that gloomy flat became a gathering place. It started with neighbors whose immediate proximity meant eye-opening conversations about daily life: why buckets of water were used to wash the floors above us thus flooding our sparse rooms with irritating regularity; cultural habits like the smells of curry and garlic or bangers and mash that wafted through the walls in early morning; where to find basic supplies, weekly markets, the fish monger. Early on, we traded for used bicycles and tricycles and, risking life and limb, learned to ride on roads overrun by overloaded bikes and car and bus traffic, all going in the "wrong" direction. There were stories of graduate studies gone awry and children struggling with schools and an English way of life.

Slowly, these exchanges expanded into conversations about what it was like living under oppressive dictatorships, third-world experiences of culture shock and sometimes survival, the immediate lack of work and purpose for women who in those days bore most of the responsibility for supporting male spouses, whose work was the reason for being there. There were lengthy discussions about religion and invitations to share Muslim holidays and Jewish holy days. Russian friends shared stories of life in post-Stalinist Russia, theirs fears and their hopes. Around our table we exchanged food and prayers and traded stories of life "at home."

To help make ends meet, I began teaching a series of classes. Women who during the day tended children and learned English came in the evening to create needlepoint samplers, puzzling over barriers of language and culture while enjoying one another's company and the creative enterprise of making something beautiful. As the groups expanded, English friends joined our multicultural experience—women from Asia and Africa, Australia and New Zealand, Europe and North and South America, all of us learning from one another and from a Jewish Prussian shopkeeper who sold us canvas, needles, and wool in his colorful Oxford shop before entertaining us in *his* Banbury Road home and regaling each group with stories of women who exchanged textile patterns along ancient "Oriental" trade routes.

"These Oxford men doing scholarly work," he'd say with unabashed disdain, "they are nothing compared to what women have done with pattern and design, with cloth and fabric and the making of homes!" And we'd laugh, pleased at his affirmations, comforted to be together in our tiny home, comforted to find here a home away from home.

On those unforgettable evenings, I often baked bread beforehand in order to quell the body smells of close quarters and different habits of hygiene. We'd eat orange rolls and cinnamon bread and drink tea while learning to know one another. The African women almost always chose bright, boldly colored skeins of wool while English friends worked with more subtle, softer hues and the Asians and Americans stitched combinations of both. I often could tell their nationalities by the colors they chose. Their names fill a book I still keep and I remember each of them with such fondness. They brought life and light and learning to our home along Banbury Road.

Finding home in England meant learning on so many levels. It was privilege and opportunity and it was life changing. For more than four years, we tended deep and lasting friendships, many of which we still treasure today. Our children learned to be curious about the bigger world and what it's like to be part of a global community. With us, they found home away from home. Even that gloomy little flat along Banbury Road became a thing of beauty, its walls hung with bright fabric, the tables filled with books, a red cyclamen gracing the window sill. It's another of our homes where life together meant sharing the holiness of ordinary things, small things and large, making our lives truly a work of art. We were at home there.

Eclectic —

REFLECTION

Home is shaped dramatically by the people who inhabit our lives. From the beginning, that gloomy flat became a gathering place. It started with neighbors whose immediate proximity meant eye-opening conversations about daily life . . .

- Which images about daily life—different cultural habits and ethnic backgrounds, food preferences, where to shop, political diversity, the challenges of graduate studies—strike you and why?

- Where have you found home away from home?

- Discuss what the holiness of ordinary things might mean for you.

6

COMING HOME TO EARTH

OTIONS ABOUT WHO AND what and where God is are powerful conceptions. Franciscan priest and writer Richard Rohr says our operative image of God is the first foundation of all religion. That working image literally shapes our understanding of ourselves and the world we inhabit and perhaps more importantly, our understanding of God. When left unexamined, this first foundation wields enormous influence over our notions of home.

You may have learned as a child—as I did—that the universe is three tiered: God's home is heaven; our home is here on earth; and a place of eternal death, hell, is the third layer or tier. Perhaps even children knew this to be only one picture in its extraordinary lack of imagination and understanding of the universe but it became a template nonetheless. This simplistically graphic picture has too often continued into adulthood, to our risk, and has encouraged an impulse to ignore or devalue the world we ought to treasure.

Taken literally, our planet was understood to be a temporary home on the way to one of the other two places. It imagined the world an undesirable place—dispensable, temporary, and expendable—a kind of transit station on the way to a God "out there" or to the underworld "down there." This one-dimensional interpretation has contributed to stunted views of God, uninformed views of an ever-expanding universe and God's place in the cosmos, and to the degradation of this stunningly beautiful planet we call home.

Literal readings of scripture that lead to undeveloped understandings of our earth home (including the ways we may read the Genesis creation stories) are wreaking havoc on this green planet. If our operative image of God creates an inclination to view the universe vertically or to reduce God to a one-dimensional "king" of the universe waiting to whisk us away from this earth, it becomes easy for us to trash the world we call home.

In our longing for home, many are looking for ways to make better sense of the mysteries of sacred identity and our place in the world. No longer able to imagine a vertical universe or to picture God in one-dimensional childhood images, we yearn to find God's face *here*, to know the presence of the Holy One in the everyday, ordinary events of our lives. We want to be grounded and connected to the earth we call home. We want to learn to love the world again, to find home here.

Coming home to earth is recognizing the kingdom of God here in this place, the spirit of the living God within us *and* without—never fully understood and part of the mystery of the inscrutable ways of the Holy One. Coming home to earth is a way of being in the world that honors intellectual integrity and accountability together with humility about all that we do not know.

Those of us who may have learned as children to picture God "out there," who worried about getting to heaven or who understood our earth home as dispensable must now face an urgently critical crisis of survival, the health of our earth. No longer can we ignore ecological concerns or make light of environmental issues or imagine a replaceable earth home or an expendable universe. Those notions have taken their toll. They come with a cost. And today as most of the world struggles to address root causes of climate change and ecological threats too numerous to list, I want us to come home to earth.

I am looking for God in the world in which we live. I want to leave behind vertical religious images to turn toward God-with-us, *here in this place.* Author Mark Brocker makes a compelling case for the importance of coming home to earth in his book of the same title, *Coming Home to Earth.*[1] The book is a radical call to Christians who have focused too long on "getting to heaven" rather than cultivating a deep love for the whole of creation. Brocker believes a loss of love for our earth home has resulted in an ecological and environmental crisis that threatens our very existence. His ardent plea to treasure and cherish our earth home points to a world and a universe created and inhabited by God.

Wrestling with who and what and where God is a lifelong challenge. I want to meet God in my neighbor and in the faces of people I might fear or dislike. I want to understand God as love and infinite compassion, a God who invites us to embody that same love and grace. I want to find God in myself—to live a God-aware life knowing the mystery and intrinsic pervasiveness of God's presence here on this earth. I want to see the wonder of God's presence in the rituals of daily routines, ordinary habits. And I want to live knowing that we are God's home and the whole world is the house of God. Coming home to earth means coming home to God. *I reassure earthly beauty.*

REFLECTION

In our longing for home, many look for ways to make better sense of the mysteries of sacred identity and our place in the world. No longer able to imagine a vertical universe or to picture God in one-dimensional childhood images, we yearn to find God's face here, to know God's presence in the everyday, ordinary events of our

---

1. Mark Brocker, *Coming Home to Earth* (Eugene: Cascade, 2016).

lives. We want to be grounded and connected to the earth we call home. We want to learn to love the world again, to find home here.

- What are some ways you might translate "coming home to earth"?

- Why or why not does "coming home to earth" mean recognizing the kingdom of God here in this place, the spirit of the living God within us *and* without—never fully understood and part of the mystery of the inscrutable ways of God?

- How might a three-tiered understanding of the universe have contributed to a lack of care for the earth?

- How do you find God in yourself? In others? How do you live a God-aware life?

7

Epiphany party

N THE MIDDLE OF our sixth decade, my spouse and I made a major move away from the home and communities we'd been part of for nearly thirty years. We were eager and we'd planned and anticipated this passage for a long time. We hoped to make it in stages, two moves half-way across the country. Our idea was that the two-part transition would be less intimidating and would satisfy our desire to be closer to our children and their families. But two moves didn't diminish the sense of loss and recurring questions of identity: Who am I now that my work has changed to something new? How do I stay connected with old friends and colleagues? Will there be new friends? Where is home?

We knew it would take time and we were keenly aware of the privilege before us. We've moved many times over the course of our lives. But this stage seemed to carry its own distinct baggage and we wanted to see it as ongoing challenge, testing, a new way of life. Dividing our time between two places—summers at the mountain cabin and winters in the Pacific Northwest—made for additional complications. Just as we began to feel at home in one community, we'd leave for the other. Why should anyone invest in friendship with people who refuse to put down roots? "Oh, you're back again—how long will you stay *this* time?" And for us: where *is* home and how do we participate in meaningful and sustained ways in two very different places?

Now six years later, I write about a recent gathering we hosted during the season of Epiphany. I write about it mainly because of the people, the friends and family who gathered with us and what their presence meant to us. For a couple of weeks, I labored over the guest list and the food preparations. My sister and her spouse, recently resettled themselves after their own cross-country move, joined us for the weekend. Who did we want them to meet and would they even enjoy a small house filled with strangers? And then the gray, dreary Epiphany afternoon began. With candles in our windows to stave off winter's darkness and to welcome friends old and new, the doorbell began to ring.

Around a colorful table laden with food and drink, we gathered to get better acquainted and to remind ourselves of friendship and camaraderie. We gathered to share the dreariness of January and some of the angst of a stage of life when physical challenges together with lifelong questions about finding home and "who am I?" are shared realities. We came together to discover connections old and new reminding all of us of our shared humanity. Lively conversation and gestures of kindness revealed similar interests, common concerns, the challenges of moving in midlife and making a new home, difficult medical diagnoses, our children and grandchildren—all of it framed by a heightened awareness of the steady ticking of time that makes life too short. Because of this, a dark and dreary afternoon was transformed into a thing of beauty.

We laughed about the penchant older people seem to have for talking about their ailments, a concession to the stark truth that our bodies are wearing out and our minds often are overwhelmed by information overload. There was a keen awareness in our gathering that we are all living one day at a time. Each of us knows the ubiquitous fears and insecurities that are our common lot. None of us has a corner on the truth or things all figured out. We all wrestle with despair and anxiety. We all know time is running out, that we are gifts to one another.

On the afternoon of the Epiphany party, it felt to me as if we'd all come home. In spite of moves from Chicago and Minnesota and Madison, in spite of the effort it takes to get acquainted and "be social," in spite of physical challenges and obvious losses, there was a tangible spirit of hope and joy, perhaps even courage. The candles brought light into the dark afternoon and the Light was present in our faces and in our words. We offered one another ourselves, the pleasure of each other's company, the generosity of our spirits.

The Epiphany party brought together people from several corners of our lives, many of them new to each other. They graced our lives and theirs by making our gathering a sacrament of belonging—to past and present places, to old and new homes, to one another. They graced our house by making it a home. Because of this, an ordinary party on a dark January afternoon was transformed into a thing of beauty. We had found home.

REFLECTION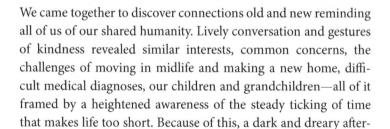

We came together to discover connections old and new reminding all of us of our shared humanity. Lively conversation and gestures of kindness revealed similar interests, common concerns, the challenges of moving in midlife and making a new home, difficult medical diagnoses, our children and grandchildren—all of it framed by a heightened awareness of the steady ticking of time that makes life too short. Because of this, a dark and dreary afternoon was transformed into a thing of beauty.

- Describe an experience you've had of leaving home or being uprooted. What was it like?

- If like me, you sometimes experience loneliness in a group, what makes a gathering feel authentic, real?

- Do you find yourself sometimes assuming that others have life all figured out or that others live lives without the anxieties you wrestle with?

- How do we make ourselves more transparent, more present?

- What makes a house a home?

8

Habitats
for humanity

IMMY AND ROSLYN CARTER's work on behalf of those without homes is legendary. With hammer and tape measure in hand and brightly colored bandanas wrapped around their heads and necks to absorb the sweat of their work and the humidity of the South, this former president and his spouse are poster children for showing people around the world the meaning of home. They have traveled the length and breadth of the United States as well as internationally helping build homes for people who until Habitat came along, could only dream of owning a house. To say Habitat for Humanity, a global housing charity now over thirty-five years old, is iconic is not an exaggeration.

Most Americans know about the Baptist peanut farmer whose rise to political fame was short-lived. This one-term president served during difficult times and was roundly criticized by his opponents. We remember descriptions of the small town he called home, some funny and not so funny stories of a family whose roots in the South were deep and strong, of religious commitments that seemed to harken from another time—teaching Sunday School and leading Bible classes and talking, acting, and talking some more about justice and what it means to care for one another. He and his family were steeped in the traditions of the South and imbued with a work ethic and moral compass that made many take notice. After leaving the White House, a house perhaps that never felt much like a home, the Carters returned to their own modest, two-bedroom ranch house, a home they'd built themselves, in Plains, Georgia. They've lived there ever since.

But theirs was not a return to obscurity or to a life lived on one's laurels or a self-conscious search for less limelight or less criticism and critiquing of what some saw as a less than successful presidency. Neither was it a return to join the speaking circuits or to cash in on notoriety. Jimmy and Roslyn Carter, both quietly committed to practicing their beliefs, continued to be activists, unrelenting voices for peace in the Middle East, passionate proponents for civil rights and human rights, for welfare reform and election monitoring. The Carter commitments are embodied in their not-for-profit, nongovernmental organization, the Carter Center in Atlanta, dedicated to waging peace, fighting disease, and building hope.

Home clearly matters to the Carters. But their definition of home far exceeds the laudable work of building houses for homeless families. Their definition of home is bigger than a quiet life in Georgia or a Sunday morning Bible study in their beloved (if sometimes conflicted) Baptist church. Their lives have focused on peaceful solutions to international conflicts, monitoring elections and advancing democracy, promoting social and economic development, caring for the earth—making home a better place for all.

If Jimmy Carter's slow, southern drawl may have sometimes seemed a bit naïve, too simple, or perhaps lacking in gravitas, don't be fooled. During his presidency he worked to establish the Panama Canal treaties, the Camp David Accords, the treaty of peace between Egypt and Israel, and the Salt II treaty with the former Soviet Union. He established the Department of Energy and supported a comprehensive energy program. He was instrumental in creating environmental protection legislation and conservation. In 2002, he was awarded the Nobel Prize for Peace.

The Carters are heroes of mine. They have responded to the world with acts of healing love and compassionate spirits. Now in their nineties and slowed only a little by age and occasional health issues, they know who they are and what it means to live meaningful lives. The Jimmy Carter whose legacy at one time looked like it might be mediocre at best is one of the great humanitarians of our time. Drawing on deep Christian roots that proclaim justice and peace for all, the Carters exemplify a multiplicity of meanings for *finding home*. They continue to live simply and to create environments that honor the earth and all its inhabitants. They respect human rights and use their voices to act on behalf of those without voices. They embody hope.

When peace and justice for all are the dual lenses for making our earth home a better place, habitats for humanity are the result. These habitats—these homes—know no borders, no walls, and no political agendas except basic human dignity. When this happens, all humanity, indeed all of creation, knows what it is to find home.

Building in Mexico

REFLECTION

Home clearly matters to the Carters. But their definition of home far exceeds the laudable work of building houses for homeless families. . . . Drawing on deep Christian roots that proclaim justice and peace for all, the Carters exemplify a multiplicity of meanings for *finding home.*

- How do you relate finding home to human rights?

- What characteristics of the Carters or others like them do you most admire?

- How do these qualities reflect Christian sensibilities and/or the best of other religious traditions?

- Reflect on a world where habitats—homes—know no borders, no walls, and no political agendas except basic human dignity.

9

Home away from home

N THE EVENING IN 2003 when the United States announced its intent to enter into war with Iraq, I sat in a dimly lit pub on the island of Crete in the Mediterranean. Gathered around a table with several Americans, Cretans, and other Greeks, we had to raise our voices to hear one another over the European commentators holding forth on the television mounted on a wall just above us. It felt as if everyone in Heraklion, indeed everyone in Greece, was ready literally to march in the streets against what they interpreted as American intervention in "their neighborhood." We Americans were upset too. The invasion of Iraq did not bode well for the Iraqis, the Middle East generally, or American standing in the world.

But around that table in a smoky room packed to the rafters with locals, our conversations went beyond the urgent fear and shock of yet another war. Many of the patrons wanted to hear what we Americans thought: "Why would your government do this in such a fragile part of the world?" "Does your president understand the complexities of the Muslim world, the centuries-long animosities between religious and political rivals, the realities of war?"

Many more discussions followed over the next weeks. The angst over our country's aggression and our willingness to listen to the Greeks created human connections and goodwill. We were able to understand their views and they ours. We could commiserate and share differences. All of us knew ourselves to be global citizens in a world desperately in need of alliances, mutuality, and trust. Everyone seemed to understand that we share a common home and we find home in the company of one another. It wasn't the first time we found home away from home.

When Mark Twain traveled through Europe in the nineteenth century, he famously wrote that travel is fatal to prejudice, bigotry, and narrow-mindedness and then added, "And many of our people need it sorely on these accounts." Those months we spent in Greece in 2003 were filled with lively discussions and experiences that made us feel at home there. Lifelong friendships were formed and though resolving the problems of the Middle East or Greece or the United States were left in limbo, we discovered our common humanity and a home away from home.

Traveling down the Mekong Delta to Vietnam from Cambodia's Tonle Sap basin recently, the grinding poverty and broken spirit of war-torn Cambodia was evident everywhere we looked. Ravaged by dictators and endless foreign intrusion, the atrocities in Cambodia have taken a toll on every aspect of this beautiful land and people. But the Cambodians we traveled with and the teachers who helped us understand their history and their suffering also showed us resilient hope and determined commitment to all that is good in their culture. A Buddhist friend who radiated inner peace and compassion even while acknowledging a world with no peace and little compassion listened to American laments and worry about our own country with authentic grace. A journalist from Phnom Penh shared hair-raising stories of carnage under Pol Pot and when we walked in the Killing Fields we all wept together. In the jungles and along the rivers of SE Asia, we discovered our common humanity and a home away from home. We were no longer strangers.

The importance of travel, whether across town or country or the world, can't be overstated. It's how we learn to navigate difference, embrace diversity, and celebrate our common humanity. Travel and genuine interest in other cultures and their people helps build relationships and a global home that benefits everyone. Getting to know immigrants and refugees makes it possible to share our own immigrant stories and struggles, acknowledging all that we do not know about one another with humility and mutuality. It opens windows and doors too often jammed shut by our prejudices and biases. It helps us find common ground and the common good, a home for all.

Rosa welcomed us to her home last spring. She didn't speak English and we were hopeless in Italian but we managed over the course of a week to communicate real friendship. With body language and facial expressions, with our eyes and ears and the help of translation apps on our phones, we could share ourselves with one another. Climbing the vertical hills to Rosa's home several times each day, we learned about her sons' wrestling feats and her family's deep roots along the Amalfi Coast. Later, we met Rosa's husband, Antonio. We tasted their homemade tomato sauce and limoncello and drank wine from the vines growing beside the house. We worshiped in their local parish and watched a procession on the Sunday after Easter that seemed to involve the entire village. We were at home there.

America's reputation in the world and its trust of our ideals is at stake. The invasion of Iraq so many years ago and today's heightened disdain for alliances continue to undermine confidence in democracy among some and respect for Islamic and Judaic and Eastern values among others. Muslims in all nations seem to believe that Iraq and its neighbors are worse off now than they were prior to 2003. Tensions around the world are growing exponentially. It isn't only our European friends and allies who are anxious about attitudes of "America first." Nationalism, isolationism, and acting only in our own interests have dangerous consequences. Yet most face-to-face encounters with neighbors around the world are affirmations of real affection for Americans, true appreciation for American generosity and spirit. Apprehension about our leadership, fears about global security, and a growing lack of trust in American policies are the downside of that affection.

Finding home away from home is vitally important. Whether traveling literally or exploring other cultures via books and media and human interactions, learning about one another *is* fatal to prejudice, bigotry, and narrow-mindedness. Finding home away from home—making home together on our planet—has never been more urgent. We all need to be able to say, *we were at home with one another.*

REFLECTION

Finding home away from home—making home together on our planet—has never been more urgent. We all need to be able to say, *we were at home with one another.*

- Describe your own experiences of learning to know strangers, perhaps in travel, perhaps in your own neighborhood.

- Do you resonate to Mark Twain's observations about travel? Why or why not?

- Why are we often fearful of those we do not know or understand?

- When have you felt yourself to be home away from home?

10

Home in the Dark of Night

OR MOST OF MY life, I have been an inveterate optimist, one who sees hope and possibility more often than sometimes makes sense. A collection of acorns sits on a shelf above my desk, reminders for me of St. Julian of Norwich's mantra, "God makes it, God loves it, God keeps it. All will be well." They've been words of comfort in difficult times but lately, the darkness has been overwhelming.

A litany of sorrow too deep for words casts a shadow over everyday life. Massacres in houses of worship, crashing planes, families wrenched apart by illness and death, young people so disillusioned with life that they take their own lives. Such darkness is of a different order than normally challenging times and it seems much darker, an aching kind of despair, impossible to comprehend.

I am not fond of seeing in *any* of these things what is sometimes referred to as "God's plan" or some other variation of "God's will." The God I continue to find compelling does not deal in despair and desolation. But this same God seems to show up even in the darkest of places—what might that be all about? Writer, priest, and teacher Barbara Brown Taylor names this kind of darkness a fear that she says "turns my knees to water" and yet she has not died nor have "monsters dragged me out of bed and taken me back to their lair." Because of this, she concludes that we learn things in the dark that are life-saving and that we seem to need darkness as much as we need light.[1]

All of us live with serious darkness in the course of our lives—there is no need to list examples—we know this to be true. But when *I* struggle with fear, when despair is nipping at *my* heels, when darkness knocks at *my* door, it's hard for me to say that I need darkness as much as light. And too often, Christians jump in with happy-clappy words, pious platitudes, or pat answers meant to comfort but lacking in genuine understanding and empathy. Might we be a little too glib about darkness, despair?

In Taylor's *Learning to Walk in the Dark*, she describes a boy who at the age of seven completely lost his sight in an accident. But his parents refused to pity him or to see his blindness as a negative and instead encouraged him to pay attention, to discover new things. Only a few days after his accident, the young boy made a discovery that captivated him for the rest of his life. While there was no doubt that his sight was completely gone, he described still being able to see light—not just a feeling or a remembrance of light, but true light in all its nuance and complexity. A few years later, he named this vivid discovery in clear and unequivocal words: ". . . I had completely lost the sight of my eyes; I could not see the light of the world anymore. Yet the light was still there, all there. . . . The source of light is not in the outer world—that's a delusion. The light dwells where life also dwells: within ourselves."[2]

When we begin to see the Holy One in our midst, in each other and in the faces of strangers, when we slowly discover *the Light that is within us*, when we know ourselves to be made in the very image and likeness of God, even darkness and fear become

1. Barbara Brown Taylor, *Learning to Walk in the Dark* (New York: HarperOne), 201, 104.

2. Taylor, *Learning to Walk*, 103–4.

vessels for bearing the Light of Christ. With the blind boy, we too can say, "I could not see the light of the world anymore—yet the light was still there." With Barbara Brown Taylor, we too look for God in the dark places. We too find home in the dark of night.

For me and perhaps for you, I find this inner Light in the liturgy of the church, in its words and music and rituals. I find it in the laments of the Psalms and in the words of honest writers, preachers, teachers. When fear and darkness seem to reign everywhere, the Light is still there. It dwells where life also dwells, within us where God dwells. For me this is finding home, knowing that even in the darkest of hours, days, or years, the mystery of the Holy One lives in that same darkness. I also understand that I truly do not understand.

In our longing to describe God, to make sense of life, to help make fear and darkness manageable and explainable, I come home to myself to discover that, mysteriously, God dwells there too. "Be still, listen, and know that I am God" says the Psalmist. And with the young boy who lost his sight, I too can say, ". . . I could not see the light of the world anymore. Yet the light was still there, all there . . . ." In the darkness of life, we find home in the Light that is within us.

REFLECTION

When fear and darkness seem to reign everywhere, the Light is still there. It dwells where life also dwells, within us where God dwells. For me this is finding home, knowing that even in the darkest of hours, days, or years, the mystery of the Holy One lives in that same darkness.

- What things have you learned in the dark that are life-saving?
- Do you agree that we seem to need darkness as much as we need light?
- Name some ways you experience inner light/Light.

- Share a psalm or another lament, perhaps from a favorite hymn—that speak meaningfully to you about fear and darkness.

- Think about the many ways we try to define God. How do you understand the mystery of God's presence?

- Do you resonate with the idea of finding home—the Light of Christ—in darkness? Why or why not?

11

Houseᴅ without homes

"ook, Nana! Why are all those tents beside the road? Over there—it's a ragged old tarp hanging from the trees! And see, there's a broken wheelchair. Look at all the garbage." Every time we drive across our stunningly beautiful city—a city, by the way, that takes pride both in its gorgeous setting and in addressing and dealing honestly with homelessness—our grandchildren are riveted by a common sight along the crisscrossing interstate highways. There are dozens of misshapen tents, broken-down cardboard boxes taped and pieced together for shelter, canvas tarps strung up for privacy and protection from the weather, and so much trash. "Why?" they ask. "Aren't they cold? It looks so wet."

And so for the hundredth time, we take a long breath and begin yet another conversation about home—making home, finding home, having no home. We began these difficult conversations when our own children were very young. Our volunteering to cook meals at the local Dorothy Day House was their first experience of sitting around tables in a homeless shelter. The house embodied the commitments of Dorothy Day, one of the founders of the Catholic Worker Movement and her single-minded attention to care for those on the margins of society. Just a couple of blocks from our own home, we walked and drove by the two-story, dilapidated brown clapboard every day. But to be inside it was another experience entirely.

We served the food and then joined the men and women and children who gathered, sometimes eagerly, often cautiously, around the tables. Conversations weren't easy. No matter how good the food or how well-intentioned our interactions might be, the palpable weight of broken bodies and damaged spirits hung heavy. In later years, a larger shelter opened and there too we took our turn, children in tow, preparing meals and sharing hospitality. One Christmas when our children were teenagers, we all celebrated Christmas Day dinner with the residents, a sobering reminder of so much of what Christmas is and isn't.

Last evening, my spouse and I found ourselves in another shelter, this one a temporary set of cloth-sided cubicles and camp cots set up in our parish hall. Four or five times a year, on a rotation with other churches in our community, we house families who are homeless while they wait for permanent, sustainable housing and employment. We made and shared the evening meal with a teenage boy (waiting for his mother to return from her job) and a young mother who'd just worked a fifteen-hour shift as a caregiver in a nursing home before picking up her eight-month-old son and two school-age children at another church where free daycare is provided for homeless families.

Homelessness is a crisis. How do we begin to explain to our young grandchildren the devastating complexities of life that lead to making one's home along the freeway under a canvas tarp or a sagging cardboard box? How do I understand the life of a twenty-something mother with three little children who cannot support herself and hasn't the resources to begin the long climb out of poverty? Why is it so easy to think of all the ways things could have been done differently, would have meant security, or might have included a home and adequate food, jobs, a better life—the "could-a, would-a, should-a"s of life?

The tangible fragility and vulnerability so visible along the interstate and in so many other places where human beings are "housed" without homes is overwhelming. I want my grandchildren to see the inequities of life and the responsibilities of privilege. I want them to feel the urgency of making the world a better place. I want them to know compassion. And as they ask their questions and puzzle over the brokenness all around us, I hope for them some anger at injustice, some indignation over what is and some determination over what should be. I want them to know that privilege creates callouses that can prevent pain. I explain how easy it is not to see. I tell them that our homes and way of life can sometimes blind us from walking in another's shoes.

Homelessness in our well-heeled city is a tragedy. But making home is not so easy. Being housed along the freeway is unthinkable. Being housed in a shelter or a church is not *finding home*. Home means more than shelter, more than a roof over vulnerable heads. Home is more than a safe place and more than a house.

May we always be uneasy about lives lived in comfort. When we grow callouses that prevent feeling empathy, may they be rubbed bare to wake us to suffering too easily ignored. May we never flinch from brokenness or turn a blind eye. May we *be* the compassionate arms of Christ, using our voices to act on behalf of those who are housed on the margins, still looking for home.

REFLECTION

Homelessness in our well-heeled city is a tragedy. But making home is not so easy. Being housed along the freeway is unthinkable. Being housed in a shelter or a church is not *finding home*. Home means more than shelter, more than a roof over vulnerable heads. Home is more than a safe place and more than a house.

- Describe what homelessness looks like in your community.

- How might you describe what it means to be housed but without a home?

- Name some ways for showing anger at injustice, indignation over what is, determination over what should be.

- Think about some less literal meanings for homelessness. What might these metaphorical meanings look and feel like in a person's search for home?

12

If you lived here . . .

 "... ou'd Be Home by Now" read quaint signs at the entrances to so many small towns and villages across the land. It's a promise one rarely sees on the outskirts of cities, where such a welcome likely would be lost in the sprawl. No, these are the words of rural life and small town communities convinced—most days—that life in their lane is preferable to just about anywhere else. A *Washington Post* reporter, Christopher Ingraham, recently published a book[1] with this title and in its fascinating pages, he tells a compelling story of his new home in rural America. Having grown up on the East Coast, he and his equally successful spouse find it increasingly difficult to make their home in the fast-paced, expensive cities of Washington, DC and Baltimore.

A data journalist, Ingraham files a story for the *Washington Post* about the ten most undesirable counties to live in the United States, citing statistics all supported by verified data. The number-one "winner" and primary subject of his research is Red Lake Falls

1. Christopher Ingraham, *If You Lived Here You'd be Home by Now* (New York: Harper, 2019).

County in Northwestern Minnesota, "the least desirable county in the entire country." Within minutes, his computer is flooded with responses from Minnesotans eager to share their views, none of them particularly angry at this East Coast foreigner so quick to pass judgment on their home, all of them bent on convincing him to "come see" what they see. Surprisingly (and not surprisingly), Ingraham's eyes-wide-open visit turns into an experience that will change the lives of his young family.

A year later after months of wrestling with this unexpected turn of life, the Ingrahams and their year-old twin sons move—lock, stock, and barrel—to Red Lake Falls, population 1,387, in the far northern reaches of Minnesota. Warm-hearted locals, eager to show them an unvarnished way of life they take for granted, help them find a home and settle into smalltown America. Of course there are ups and downs, highs and lows, suspicion about East Coast writers, misunderstandings. But what this family discovers in the expansive prairie of the Upper Midwest is an embracing community ready to welcome and care for one another, a community at home with itself.

Never mind winter's guarantee of snow measured in feet and record-breaking temperatures. Ignore the lack of restaurants, a limited inventory of small shops and grocers, and the inevitable fact of everyone knowing everyone else's business. Embrace instead a slower pace of life, wide open spaces and the beauty of nature, and gracious people ready to disprove the singular power of statistics by welcoming and befriending even their most famous critic.

The story of the Ingrahams is poignant for me. I too was transplanted in the Midwest and spent several decades of my life living in Minnesota, both as a child and later on with my own family. I learned to find beauty in its landscape and drama in winter blizzards and sub-zero temperatures. Even so, my longing for home in the Pacific Northwest went unabated and I have written often about bleakly cold winters on the flat undulating prairie. But I too found home there. Not far from Red Lake Falls, my immigrant great-grandfather served a country parish, his gravesite marking his Minnesota home alongside many other family members buried in that place. My West Coast grandmother who moved from her beloved Minnesota as a young woman never made her peace with the damp climate of Puget Sound or the green, mossy winters in the shadow of the Cascade Mountains. Still, she too was at home in the Pacific Northwest.

Home in many places is not an uncommon story. I remember the wrenching move away from the home of my childhood. It was about geography and familiarity, family loyalty, and the roots of my life. Pulling those roots up to reveal their tenacious hold was not easy. But of course the roots were never severed. I carried them with me to be replanted in new soil, grafted into new life. It was the first of many later moves, each one opening doors and windows I could not have envisioned or imagined.

Where is home for you? Are there multiple places where you feel the comforting familiarity of home? Why do you live where you do? What do you expect of home? How do you go about making home? Have you ever thought about finding home somewhere else? Is there a place where you might longingly say, "If I lived here, I'd be home by now?"

Home is a central biblical theme. The creation story tells of the Holy One making home in a garden among all the creatures God has created. The entire biblical narrative describes the many ways God makes a home, abides with us and, for Christians, becomes incarnate in the person of Jesus. At the end of Christian scripture, the writer of Revelation promises a lasting home, a new Jerusalem. In the mystery and enigmatic nature of the biblical stories, I find another home. Not etched in stone, not always with sharply defined features or a corner on truth, not always cozy or in one place but home nonetheless.

What constitutes the goodness of home? The Ingrahams found a way of life that made more of them—more space, more time, genuine friendship, meaningful engagement in community life. I expect home to be a place for embrace and joy, for shelter and meaning. More than happiness, home is where I discover again and again who I am, who my neighbor is, and what matters most to both of us. Finding home in the world and knowing ourselves to be God's home means I live here. It means I am home.

REFLECTION

Home is where I discover again and again who I am, who my neighbor is, and what matters most to both of us—a place for embrace and joy, for shelter and meaning.

- Describe a place you've always thought of as home.
- Is there a place you've sometimes longed to call home? Why?
- What do you expect of home?
- What constitutes the goodness of home for you?

13

Imago Dei

T WAS AN ORDINARY Sunday afternoon but I shall never forget its poignancy. I sat on the bed in our upstairs bedroom. My mother lived faraway and we were sharing yet another long-distance phone conversation. She was deep in the throes of depression, barely able to make coherent sentences, desperate for help. Her voice was soft and so far away that I had to strain to hear her. Even today, more than a decade later, I feel her desperation and the weight of her angst.

To calm her and to comfort myself, I kept reminding her of a loving God who would not abandon her. Over and over again, I described the grace she'd shared with me as a child, overwhelming and unconditional love, a God who suffers with us and for us, and most of all, a God who makes us in God's own image.

But her darkness was too deep, too profound, and imago Dei was not a theological concept she could experience for herself. She'd lost her eyesight a few years earlier. She and my father struggled through several midlife crises. She was smart and capable and would have found fulfillment in a vocation or profession perhaps more defining than homemaking and child-rearing or being the spouse of a pastor. Physical losses became a regular source of frustration and her generation of women often felt limited, even trapped, in expectations that too often discouraged the pursuit of their own dreams and ambitions.

Maybe most of all, the very words of grace she'd offered in my childhood—"You, dear child! You are made in the image of God!"—belied her depression-induced default: "lowly-worm" Protestant piety that seemed to fall hardest on her own deafened ears. My mother's well-meaning parents, whose lives were shaped by this same Protestant piety ("be careful about thinking too highly of yourself" or "don't get the big head!"), who made sure their sons went to university but lacked the wisdom to encourage their only daughter in similar pursuits, were overly protective—no doubt in part because my mother's twin sister had died as an infant. It all took a toll.

And so in desperation on that ordinary Sunday afternoon, I began to sing across the miles to my mother—perhaps mostly for my own aching heart but also as a way of surrounding her with hope and love.

> "Healer of our every ill, light of each tomorrow, give us peace beyond our fear, and hope beyond our sorrow . . ."

> "The king of love my shepherd is, whose goodness fails me never . . ."

> "Eat this bread, drink this cup, taste and see the goodness of God . . ."[1]

At one time or another, many of us struggle with the crippling implications of "lowly-worm" theology: an overwhelming sense of brokenness, powerlessness, vulnerability. My tradition is deeply influenced by St. Augustine's interpretations of original sin and it's hard for us to grasp the life-changing and life-challenging inferences of being made in the image of God. A God of judgment somehow reinforces our own need to judge—others as well as ourselves. This is not to say we are without sin or that we are perfect

---

1. Hymns from *Evangelical Lutheran Worship* (Minneapolis: Augsburg Fortress, 2006).

like God. What it does say is that God's image, imago Dei, is our inherent identity. In the opening chapter of Genesis, God spoke us into being, "Let us make humans in our image, according to our likeness."

Why is God's love for the world—God's love for us—so difficult to fathom? Without minimizing the crippling illness of clinical depression as a medical reality, too many of us suffer from an inability to grasp the implications of being made in God's own image. The overwhelming love of God together with the generative nature of God, always creating, resurrecting, and restoring life, embodies everything God is.

To be created in God's image means we are in union with God. God makes God's home in us. We ourselves are invited to embody God, to be little Christ's. We are God's home and the whole world is the house of God, our literal physical and spiritual home. On that Sunday afternoon as I sang to my mother over the phone, I wanted her to feel God's presence within her. I wanted her to know the shelter and the security of God's overwhelming love. I desperately wanted her to see and to feel at home in her own arms and in the arms of God.

The disease of depression finally robbed my mother of those assurances. Nevertheless, she knew the literal and spiritual meanings of home and passed along to me the deep awareness of a God whose grace and love and sense of justice is so deep and so ubiquitous as to create us in the Holy One's very image. This gift of God's grace and unconditional love is hard for us to fathom. God's image, imago Dei, is our inherent identity. It is, in the words of Catholic theologian Matthew Fox, our original blessing and it is our true home. Thanks be to God!

REFLECTION

To be created in God's image means we are in union with God. God makes God's home in us. We ourselves are invited to embody God, to be little Christ's. . . . I wanted my mother to feel God's presence, to know the shelter and the security of God's overwhelming love. I desperately wanted her to see and to feel at home in her own arms and in the arms of God.

- Why is God's love for the world—God's love for us—so difficult to fathom?

- Have you or someone you know experienced the crippling implications of "lowly-worm" theology? What are some manifestations?

- What does imago Dei mean to you?

- Too many suffer from an inability to grasp the implications of being made in God's own image. The overwhelming love of God together with the generative nature of God, always creating, resurrecting, and restoring life embodies everything God is. How do we live the Love that God is?

14

In the shelter of each other

MONG THE MEMORIES I treasure most are the years my family and I lived in England. Our children were young, a third daughter born just before we returned home, and we were embarking on an adventure we could not yet see all that clearly. We knew the rigors of graduate school would be daunting; we expected to live simply and without many material privileges or comforts; and we hoped for a circle of friends, a community that would help us adapt to a new way of life so far from home and family. Those years and many of the details of our Oxford home are described more fully in "Banbury Road," another of the chapters in this book.

The years in England were highlighted by the many ways a wide swath of people became intricately woven into our lives. It was an in-between time, a bridge between one world and another. And in that particularly formative period of our lives, a heightened awareness of "in-between" and "not yet" meant we needed each other's care more than ever. English friends whose seemingly more settled lives made us envious opened their hearts and shared their homes, many becoming lifelong friends. In the university community people came and went with painful regularity and through it all we discovered shelter, not only in the arms of our small family, but in the embrace of so many others. We found home in one another.

Our forebears—our ancestors—no doubt experienced something similar as they emigrated from one land to another to make a new home. Whether life in the old country was without a future, family circumstances painful, or the lure of the new world a talisman of hope and promise—realistic or not, they came knowing it wouldn't be easy, that hardships would challenge every hard-fought gain, that loneliness would sometimes be unbearable. On remote prairie homesteads and in hard-scrabble depression-era towns, they worked to create a new life, begin families, and build homes, finding shelter in one another, welcoming and supporting each other through difficult times.

For many years my sisters and I have taken time away from our spouses and homes to travel together. At first it was to help us cope with the circumstances of our aging parents and their difficult end-of-life challenges. After their deaths, we traveled to Scandinavia where we explored places new and old, visiting family along the way. But yearly short jaunts with my sisters have been simply for the pleasure and necessity of spending time together. Of course there are a thousand things to share—who has known us as long as a sibling? But mostly we gather to be in each other's good company, to find shelter in each other, to find home together. Neighbors and friends and colleagues also have been part of regular gatherings, sharing similar interests, helping one another cope with frightening medical diagnoses, challenging life circumstances, parenting teenagers into adulthood, and so much more. We find shelter in one another, wings to help us fly, and nets to catch our sometimes sagging spirits.

When I reread old journals or occasionally visit with long-time friends, I'm reminded of the fact that there has never been a time without worry, agonizing angst, or anxiety of one kind or another. Writing today, we are living through a political crisis that threatens the fabric of our democracy.[1] Many are justifiably fearful that the rule of law has been undermined, that corruption has seeped into the souls of too many in positions of power, and that the American experiment in democracy so respected around the world may not be able to regain balance and authority.

I share these worries with many and on especially bad days we hold one other in a circle of companionship and camaraderie, providing shelter for each other. Some days it feels as if we live in the flimsy houses of the three little pigs with a band of wolves at the door ready to burn them all down. We need to make a strong home together, not with straw or sticks, maybe not even with bricks. The home we share on this planet is in dire need of ecological balance and care. Antipathy in our own land has been used to divide and set us against each other, not only here but around the world. There may be no more important task before us than relearning what it means to belong to one another, to share a common home, to think communally and globally, for the common good and for the sake of the world.

African cultures have a word for this: *Ubuntu*. It means that we live in the shelter of each other. It means that *I am because we are*. It means that *we are because Christ is*. It means we do life together! It is in the shelter of each other that we find a common home. It doesn't take long to discover that "going it alone" is not a good way to live. We need one another. We do indeed do life together!

REFLECTION

It is in the shelter of each other that we find a common home, . . . going it alone is not a good way to live. We need one another because we do indeed do life together!

- Name some places where you are especially aware of being cared for by others.

1. The tenure of Donald Trump as president of the United States that began in 2016 was fraught with crises.

- Describe an experience of community where you have felt the shelter of others.

- What keeps you going when worry and anxiety seem to threaten daily life?

- Do you agree that there may be no more important task before us than relearning what it means to belong to one another, to share a common home, to think communally and globally, for the common good and the sake of the world?

15

Mysteries
of Existence

T was another afternoon at a shelter for families without a permanent home. We'd brought dinner and others would come to spend the evening, hoping for conversation, news of a possible apartment becoming available, hope for a change in fortune. One young woman was six months pregnant with twins, her partner doting affectionately as we asked questions about the babies. Leroy, a little boy about seven or eight years old, ran frantically from person to person, back and forth over and over again, a graphic picture of anxiety and agitation. Others sat glassy-eyed, waiting for the evening meal.

In the unforgettable novel, *Lila*, Pulitzer Prize-winning author Marilynne Robinson tells the story of a girl abandoned as a baby and rescued as a toddler by a warm hearted vagabond, herself wounded and homeless.[1] Together they make their way in the shadows of fear, uncertainty, and aching loneliness, living among other wanderers all struggling to exist. Yet in spite of their fragile

1. Marilynne Robinson, *Lila* (New York: Picador, 2014).

existence, there are moments of acute wonder, occasional joy, a hunger for knowledge that leads to learning to read, and a keen observation of life outside the furthest edges of society.

Some years later and now a young woman, Lila wanders into a church in a small Iowa town looking for shelter from a rainstorm. She finds there a solitary pastor whose authenticity, humility, and kindness are curiosities of the highest order. Prompted along the way by his preaching and his own lonely solitude, Lila and John Ames begin a starkly real and oddly believable web of conversations about the meaning of life, eventually learning to love each other, and then to marry. The incongruity and absurdity of their match is never downplayed and Lila will spend the rest of her life trying to make sense of abandonment and loss and the overwhelming love of a gracious God embodied in John Ames. Their story is a moving expression of profound woundedness and the mysteries of existence.

The story of *Lila* has haunted me just as every experience among displaced and dispossessed people in my own life haunts me. What is the meaning of existence? Lila would press John Ames with "You [was] talking about it all the time and I didn't know what it means—I had to learn that word, existence." Leroy, the little boy in the family shelter, might have said the same thing. His family was evicted two days later, perhaps because his behavior was so disruptive, perhaps because his family could not make sense of that word, existence.

The search for meaning is universal whether we know the word existence or not. The lives of Lila and Leroy illustrate the harshness of the world and a sometimes desperate struggle for survival and meaning, for home and love and security. Yet trying to get at the essence of a deep longing to understand existence can hardly be captured in a book or a paragraph or an image. Where is a loving God in such suffering?

I do not know what to say about Leroy, living this week in a temporary shelter, last week in another makeshift "home," next week who knows where! He likely has spent the majority of his short life in an endless cycle of neglect and insecurity. His wounded soul and spirit are written across his face and in the frantic movements of his body. How does one make sense of such brokenness? A warm meal and protection from the night seem ludicrous in the face of so much want, such desperation. Where are you, O God, in *this* child's life?

And with trepidation I share the luminous writing of a novelist who faces similar questions. I do so because this author has an uncanny sense of the incongruities of life. She is a narrator of the realities of the human condition and an interpreter of the miracle of existence. She speaks the wordlessness we feel as we watch life unfold, holding on for dear life to those we love and to mysteries we cannot understand. She knows the solitary loneliness that characterizes our lives. She knows the hidden face of God on the edges of everyday existence—and sometimes front and center if only we could see.

Such a grand phrase, *the meaning of existence,* and such a hopeful title, *Finding Home.* Is existence really a miracle or is it the luck of the draw that too often becomes a life sentence? What is it like to live on the streets? Where are you, O God, in the searing pain of abandonment and abuse? Does God dwell *there*? And what does God expect of us in the face of such adversity? What does my life mean? Where *is* home?

I want to see the face of Christ in the shelter where we share a meal, in the faces of those with whom we break bread, in my own brokenness. We spend a lifetime trying to make sense of things: who God is and what God is like, what to do with unspeakable suffering, what our own existence means and why every life matters, what it is that keeps us going. May the hidden face of the Holy One be at the center of all these queries and may we ourselves be the not-so-hidden face of Christ, bearing hopeful witness to a loving and gracious God even as we wrestle with the mysteries of existence and with what it means to find home.

REFLECTION

I want to see the face of Christ in the shelter where we share a meal, in the faces of those with whom we break bread, in my own brokenness. We spend a lifetime trying to make sense of things: who God is and what God is like, what to do with unspeakable suffering, what our own existence means and why every life matters, what it is that keeps us going. May the hidden face of the Holy One be at the center of all these queries and may we ourselves be the not-so-hidden face of Christ, bearing hopeful witness to a loving and gracious God even as we wrestle with the mysteries of existence and with what it means to find home.

- How do you make sense of the hidden face of God?
- Where is God in the searing pain of abandonment and abuse?
- Where does God dwell and what does God expect of us?
- What keeps you going?
- Consider reading *Lila* and Marilynne Robinson's earlier book, *Gilead*.

16

No crib for a bed

N MY TRADITION, AMONG the first hymns of Christmas learned by children is a nineteenth-century text, "Away in a Manger." Whether one knows the earlier melody or prefers (as I do) a later arrangement by English composer Sir David Willcocks, the lyrics and music illustrate a hauntingly iconic image of the birth of the Christ child—far from home in a manger stall meant for animals because there was no room anywhere else. There was *no crib for his bed.*

As a very young child just learning the meaning of home, I imagined this image by creating a manger in an old hollowed out tree stump outside our home in the mountains of Western Washington. In that soft cradle of leaves and moss and pine needles, I spent hours playing with my doll—making for her a bed and a home, a manger in a rotted stump. Even as a three-year old, there was some latent awareness of the pathos of not having a home, of *no crib for a bed.*

These days, it is not a stretch for us to picture fleeing families, young children and babies in tow, and yes, pregnant mothers risking their lives as they seek safety, asylum, and shelter for themselves and the people they love. Their struggle to escape unspeakable circumstances is recorded for posterity in a world where cameras and television and daily news cycles record it all, making palpable the pain and grief and fear that cannot be ignored. We see their faces and hear their voices with almost daily regularity.

Perhaps for the first time, these graphic images of refugees and immigrants—of children separated from their parents—have been seared into the collective psyche of many in our own land, poignant reminders of fear and desperation most of us cannot begin to fathom. But of course such suffering goes beyond our own time and our own borders. Whether in Syria or Palestine or Somalia or thousands of other places around our globe where there is *no crib for a bed*, we are painfully aware of a world seemingly unable to provide safety, security, and a way of life everyone on this planet deserves.

For Christians, the coming of Christmas is an invitation to embrace a child without a home, without a bed. As in nearly all world religions, we are charged with shared responsibility for the vulnerable. We are asked to pay attention, to feed the hungry, care for the poor, visit those in prison, protect all who flee for their lives. Ensconced as we sometimes are in the comforts of our culture, it's a challenge to pay attention and engage with those who have no bed. Our frenetic buying and often frivolous preparations for Christmas—together with the privilege most of us enjoy the rest of the year—have little to do with the coming of Christ.

For many living in what we sometimes rather arrogantly call the first world, our own circumstances can blind us to making room in the inn, a soft place in the hay, a shelter for all who flee oppression, persecution, and tyranny. What does it mean to make room for the Christ child? What does it look like to make room, a home, a bed for the family living on the streets? How might *we* become conduits of compassion and kindness, unconditional acceptance and grace? How might we become home for those with no home?

In the tradition where I find home, Christmas is a homecoming. Like many other religious celebrations, it asks us to take stock of our own broken lives and self-preoccupation by focusing on a newborn child. This child we call Jesus is on display around the world and in our own neighborhoods. This newborn without a bed and without a home contains the mystery of the Holy One, an invitation to see our own neediness and vulnerability in the faces of every broken life. This child without a bed asks us to put aside all the distracting and befuddling obsessions of our culture to make space for the mystery of God, the very presence of Christ. It asks us to make room for a crib big enough to cradle God's love and grace for all.

Christmas is about seeing the face of God in all the forgotten faces and broken places, hearing God's heartbeat in our own beating hearts. It's about making space—accommodations—for strangers, those who know no home, those with *no crib for a bed*. Christmas is a way of coming home, finding home, being home. In Christian parlance, "the Word became flesh and dwelt among us" means that God dwells in us. God makes God's home in us.

> *Christ is the path and Christ is the door. Christ is the bread*
> *and welcome cup. Christ is the word and cleansing bath.*
> *Christ is the robe and Christ is the fire. Christ is the dawn*
> *and blazing sun. Christ is the light and Christ is the star.*
> *Christ is the beginning and the end. Christ is our life and*
> *Christ is our home.*[1]

The living God is in our midst, making God's home among us. Christ is our life and Christ is our home.

REFLECTION

It is not a stretch for us these days to picture fleeing families, young children and babies in tow, and yes, pregnant mothers risking their lives as they seek safety, asylum, and shelter for themselves and the people they love.

1. Poem used with permission from author Samuel Torvend, Pacific Lutheran University.

- What does it mean to make room in the inn, a soft place in the hay, shelter for all who flee oppression, persecution, tyranny?

- If we believe that the Word became flesh and dwelt among us, what then might it mean that God makes God's home in us?

- *No crib for a bed* has so many meanings. How might you interpret this for yourself? For others?

- How do your celebrations of holy days and holidays reflect what it means to see the face of God in all the forgotten faces and broken places?

17

Our deep gladness, the world's deep need

RIVING THE LABYRINTHINE STREETS of our city one morning before dawn, I was struck by the many office windows where, under bright lights, people obviously were already working. The warmth of the lights in the dark of early morning and the images of people absorbed at their desks—computer screens lit up, cups of coffee in hand, phones to their ears—were striking. While most of the city slept, here they were seemingly at home in offices and cubicles, work spaces both large and small. They may have been working nightshifts, avoiding city traffic, enjoying flexible scheduling, or simply working long hours—all possibilities. But as I gazed across the maze of freeways at the tall buildings that morning, I imagined people whose workplace was also a second home.

There is no doubt that it may have been a graphic picture of the long hours most people *have* to work. Neither is there any doubt that work can be so consuming and demanding that it may as well serve as a home—so much time is spent at it. But what I saw that morning was work as *vocation*, a *calling*, the place "where our deep gladness meets the world's deep need," writer Frederick Buechner's classic quote about God's call to meaningful work. That morning in Portland, I imagined a few privileged people for whom the satisfaction of work transforms it into another kind of home. Once out of the city and in rolling rural countryside, another image flashed in front of me: an old dilapidated barn framed by fenced fields and a small farm house set against the slopes of the foothills. The lights in the farmhouse windows also burned brightly and I visualized a family inside getting ready for morning chores, feeding and caring for animals, working in the fields, perhaps getting ready to go to school. What was their home like? Did the work of the farm or the fact of a day at school count as fulfilling labor? Was the farm a welcomed way of life or an unending source of tiringly hard work? Biblical stories sometimes portray work as a curse, citing a God who punishes or masters and servants for whom work is akin to slavery. Perhaps the farm felt like that.

And what about work that is demeaning, underpaid? What about the insecurity of no work? Driving through the city earlier, I had only to look another direction to observe the realities of homelessness and joblessness. Might work of any kind, let alone fulfilling work, be an expectation of privilege, an entitled assumption of class and circumstances?

How does one find a sense of home at the core of their work? Is it merely satisfaction? Success with difficult tasks? Getting the job done? Or are we trying to unearth something deeper: finding our selves in a vocation, in work that brings together interests and passions and expertise with the needs of others and the needs of the world. Is that too grand an expectation? Naïve optimism? Privileged talk? What *does* meaningful work look like and for whom?

Finding home in one's work *is* deep gladness. It describes work as an expression of wholeness, work you most need to do and work the world most needs to have done. Christians often speak about it as vocation—from the Latin, *vocare*, work one is called to by God. I think of it as work that makes daily life holy and ordinary existence sacred. I understand finding home in one's work as the extraordinary good fortune of meshing what one loves with what one does.

I still dream about the work I did for several decades: writing, recommending resources, helping leaders find the best teaching tools, collecting and evaluating books and authors, curricula, media. I was a teacher and I relished the art of resourcing and mentoring. That work clearly is deep in my psyche, just sleepy nods away from an ongoing life of its own—reminding me regularly how much I miss its challenges, the interactions with people I love and respect, the life-giving satisfaction it brought. It was holy work, work as vocation, work as finding home.

Together with my spouse, my work is also the making of a home. For me, this homemaking always has been another vocation as well as an art. It is deeply satisfying, a way of hallowing the ordinary and finding home in one's work, of making daily life something more than tasks to be finished, meals to be made, children to be cared for, mundane duties. It is not commonplace or quotidian.

Whether harvesting crops as a migrant worker, driving the city's sanitation trucks to collect garbage, practicing law enforcement, or working in a downtown office in the dark of night, work is holy. It allows us to be co-creators with God. When sweeping streets or waiting tables or caring for children expresses one's commitments and longings for making the world a better place, each becomes sacramental, conveying something more than a product or a service. When someone finds home in the work they do, that work is transformed into a thing of beauty.

So with a healthy dose of humility and an acknowledgement of my own privilege and inclination to see the world through optimistic eyes, I want to celebrate *work* and *home* as one: work as an expression of wholeness and home as the extraordinary good fortune of meshing what one loves with what one does. Finding home in one's work is deep gladness indeed!

REFLECTION

Finding home in one's work *is* deep gladness. It describes work as an expression of wholeness, work you most need to do and work the world most needs to have done. Christians often speak about work as vocation . . . I think of it as that which makes daily life holy and ordinary existence sacred. I understand finding home in one's work as the extraordinary good fortune of meshing what one loves with what one does.

- How does one find a sense of home at the core of one's work?

- How might work of any kind, let alone fulfilling work, be an expectation of privilege, an entitled assumption of class and circumstances?

- What does it mean to find oneself in a vocation, in work that brings together interests and passions and expertise with the needs of others and the needs of the world? Is this too grand an expectation? Is it naïve optimism, privileged talk?

- What *does* meaningful work look like and for whom?

18

Politics?
BRING IT ON . . . !

INDING MY POLITICAL HOME was not an easy feat. Perhaps that is true for most of us. Though I would like to think I was somehow shaped politically "in utero" by the world my grandparents experienced during the Great Depression, that isn't likely. In those extraordinarily difficult years, my grandparents depended on leaders like Franklin Roosevelt (and a bit more reservedly, Eleanor Roosevelt) whose courage and farsightedness helped Americans recover from very dark days. The prescience and compassion of the Roosevelt administration was about improving people's lives.

In the years following the Great Depression, landmark legislation guaranteed the social security we still depend on today. Newly created jobs finally began to make employment a reality and food stamps and other social services literally saved many Americans in their struggle to survive. "Politics" was about finding concrete ways to improve people's lives by sharing the ideals of democracy—peacemaking, economic justice, and a fair chance for all. The Democratic Party of the Roosevelts took those ideals seriously. So did my grandparents. They understood politics to be about protecting people by governing with compassionate responsibility. Agencies were created to work for equity and justice. After the searing experiences of war and depression-era poverty, our nation was hungry for peace and a better way of life for all.

As more prosperous times returned, both political parties gained momentum. Family members became active in local government, serving on the school board and in a county position, running for and being elected to state office, even a close run for governor of the state of Washington. Somewhere along the way Democrats came to be associated with irresponsible spending, the wrongs of "big government," and the dreaded word, liberalism. That turning point for my family meant embracing the Republican Party, which seemed to extol conservative values including a Republican understanding of free market capitalism and what they interpreted as too much government and too many taxes.

Political discussions happened at most family gatherings and especially during election years. We were fiscal conservatives who too easily slipped into broad generalizations about the poor, suspicion of government programs, and rigid notions of individualism. Social justice and care of the neighbor got short shrift. In those days, the Republican Party seemed to care most about main street businesses and a strong economy while the Democrats were often portrayed as "bleeding heart" liberals lacking common sense about responsible governmental limits. The long and the short: I grew up thinking Barry Goldwater and Richard Nixon were trustworthy, responsible leaders.

It did not take long as a university student to see cracks in my firmly held notions of good government and bad. They began to crumble in part because of religious questions: What does it mean to be my neighbor's keeper? Why did Jesus associate with the poor, the outcast, people who were socially unacceptable? Is there such a thing as just war? I was studying the liberal arts in a university committed to social issues, to peace and justice. We were expected to participate in college groups dedicated to helping impoverished communities around the city. Angry demonstrations against the

Vietnam War had become common place. The Kent State massacre of students protesting the bombing of Cambodia shocked us all and we'd been stunned by Martin Luther King, Jr.'s assassination.

Religious questions began to merge into political questions and as a result, the political questions became central to the faith I professed. I do not want to glorify the process or claim some pious awakening or espouse simplistic notions of political identity. But the complications of American individualism, economics, and exceptionalism no longer rang true.

It was a dramatic turn that only gained momentum as I found my own voice and listened to the world around me. No doubt much about finding a political home is classic coming-of-age identity development—mine did not please my family. And just as religious questions had been the impetus for rethinking political identity as a young student, the church and my adult understandings of biblical injunctions were central in this unfolding process of finding a political home.

Does finding one's political home mean unquestioned loyalty to a partisan list of issues and unswerving support for one party? That would be the epitome of ignorance and arrogance. But through all the intervening years, I have found trustworthy intersections connecting my political and religious commitments. I continue to relish political conversations and the passion and engagement they require. I am grateful for lifelong work in a church body unafraid of controversy and willing to speak and act publicly on behalf of the voiceless, the oppressed, the poor. The prophetic voices of the church and its corporate nature as the sacrificial Body of Christ help shape my commitments. This interrelatedness of faith, politics, and religious obligations undergirds and enhances the sense of knowing my political home.

Today's stark images of bitter political partisanship, widespread corruption, and unchecked nationalism and individualism make former times seem tame and perhaps more noble. But selective memory is dangerous and of course politics has never been tame or blameless. With today's frontrow seats in the theater of national and global political maneuvering, it's more important than ever to pay close attention to politics gone awry. We need to be vigilant about fact checking and wary of fear mongering. Finding a political home requires acknowledging one's own myopia as well as listening to trustworthy voices of wisdom while responding with generosity and compassion, humility and grace. It's a lifelong challenge finding one's political home—no small feat indeed!

REFLECTION

Does finding one's political home mean unquestioned loyalty to a partisan list of issues and unswerving support for one party? That would be the epitome of ignorance and arrogance. But I have found trustworthy intersections connecting my political and religious commitments. The prophetic voices of the church and its corporate nature as the sacrificial Body of Christ continue to give me hope, direction, and the courage to be politically engaged.

- How might you define the meanings of finding a political home?

- Name some voices that give you hope and the courage to speak and act politically.

- What is your experience of the interrelatedness of faith, politics, and religious commitments?

- Why is it important to have a political home?

19

QUESTIONS OF FAITH

If God is your answer to every question, eternal and absolute,
once-and-for-all kind of answer, without a doubt,
no wondering, dithering, or hypothesizing,
no clever juggling,
struggling, pondering, or agonizing;
no raised eyebrow or pursed lips,
no tilted head with faraway gaze—
just straight out, eyes glazed,
one syllable,
constant and unequivocal,
you smiling, smiling, always smiling
sweetly to every question:
God.
Then,
all questions vanish,
all questions perish,
and you stand like a post
from one of your fences,
not even enough of you
for the upright of a cross

Questions of Faith

like one Jesus chose at the end,
facing death, and desperately
asking the ultimate question:
God, where are you?
And hearing nothing,
resigned to silence,
said, Nevertheless, I AM
and died the Lamb
still with his question.
Now there's an answer,
God.[1]

 OD, WHERE ARE YOU? Some days it seems as if there are almost no glimpses, no intimation or tiniest glimmer, no inkling whatsoever of where you are or what you might be. On those days when the consuming wreckage of life is strewn as far as the eye can see and doubt and disappointment come like tsunami waves destroying everything in their path, no amount of pious speculating or definitive statements of faith can penetrate the gaping hole of *not knowing*.

Questions of faith? Oh yes! My faith tradition claims rigorous intellectual commitments together with taking the lead to question practices of sixteenth-century Catholicism and help birth the Protestant Reformation. Together with the best of Catholicism— sacramental life, high regard for mystery and symbolism, practicing justice, and a robust liturgical sensibility—the Reformation has shaped and honed my question-driven faith.

Coming from a long line of questioners and a church that continues to make the case for ongoing reform, I chafe over much of what has come to define a life of faith. I'm uncomfortable with neat definitions and binary simplicities that tether us to our particular corners on the truth. I am wary of fences made to keep

1. Warren L. Molton, "If God Is Your Answer." *Christian Century*, June 14, 2004.

others out, of becoming a post in one of those fences. I am anxious about the ease with which we make faith claims for our brand of religion, our particular doctrines and creeds, our unique world-views. I want to be careful about reducing the mysteries of who God is and what God is like to our place in history or our limited understandings of the universe, science, even notions of the beginning and ending of time.

Yes, we see through contextual eyes and yes, every generation makes sense of questions of faith for their historical setting. But I want to find my faith home in an expansive understanding of God that is more welcoming of questions than insistent on lines in the sand. I cannot claim the truth, the way, and the life unless those ways embrace all of creation with the extravagant love and compassion I attribute to God. I want to confess my feeble attempts to understand Jesus in the larger context of a cosmic Christ who didn't just arrive in the world 2,000+ years ago as a babe but has existed since the beginning of time, the spirit of Christ that permeates every created thing. When the story of the Nativity in my tradition leaves room for mystery and opens our eyes to the wonder of the Holy One embodied in Jesus, doors and windows open into a universe we cannot begin to grasp.

That universe includes my Buddhist friends and Muslim neighbors seeking God in contexts different from mine. It includes the earth we call home and all its creatures, a mind-blowing exhibition of the generosity and generativity of God. It includes all that we do not know and cannot see. God's presence in the world is found where justice and equity flourish, where every human life and every created thing is treated with dignity and care, where a child shows us the face of the Holy One and where loving the world means giving away one's life so that others may live, where strangers are welcomed home and prisoners set free.

It's that kind of God in which I want to find home, a God present in all cultures and civilizations, a God of overwhelming love, mercy, justice, and peace. Might God be the house in which we find home—doors flung wide in welcome, light spilling from every window, a shelter and a refuge, graced spaciousness? In the largess of this home with all its open doors and windows, places are made for the hungry, the lost, the broken, the weary. Extravagant love is poured out for all and in the coming and going of the seasons, new life is celebrated and old life is honored. This is the home I teach my children to love and to protect. This is the home where God dwells.

So let us make the opening wide to look for a God who is still being revealed. Let us ask a thousand questions. Let us discover new ways for thinking about the Holy One, the great *I AM*. Let us know ourselves to be made in God's image, the *I am* that answers the question, who am I? Let us find joy in our differences and peace in our shared humanity. We are God's dwelling place. We are God's home and the whole world is the house of God. Finding home indeed!

REFLECTION

I chafe over much of what has come to define a life of faith. I'm uncomfortable with neat definitions and binary simplicities that tether us to our particular corners on the truth. I am anxious about the ease with which we make faith claims for our brand of religion, our particular doctrines and creeds, our unique world-views. I want to be careful about reducing the mysteries of who God is and what God is like . . . .

- Might God be the house in which we find home—doors flung wide in welcome, light spilling from every window, a shelter and a refuge, graced spaciousness? Does this make sense to you? Why or why not?

- What does it mean to you that God continues to be revealed?

- Where do you find space for questions of faith?

- Consider reading Richard Rohr' daily posts at www.cac.org

20

Refugees Looking for Home

OME TIME AGO, I had an unsettling experience seeing photographs of sculptures by French artist Bruno Catalano (http://brunocatalano.com/). Those sculpted images of the hollowed-out bodies of refugees fleeing their homes, identities, and cultures are seared into my psyche. As often happens with extraordinary art, the graphic essence of broken lives is depicted more powerfully than all the words and photos and stories we use to make sense of such tragedy. Looking at them I was dumbstruck by the weight of the losses and the sheer absence of identity, the depth of which I could not imagine.

Catalano's life-sized sculptures are gouged out semblances of bodies, hauntingly empty spaces where organs and muscle and flesh once were, heads intact as they stride away from wherever and whatever "home" might have been. My visceral reaction to the powerful sense of loss conveyed in Catalano's work still takes my breath away.

Nearly forty years ago, my family helped resettle Uoc and Bay, a couple in their early twenties who arrived in the United

States shell-shocked by their tortuous journey from Vietnam. They had left their small village where news of the world, let alone the United States, was practically non-existent and then spent months in an overcrowded refugee camp. The couple came with two small children and with Bay's younger sister and her husband. None of them spoke any English. None of them were literate in their own language. They were simply and not so simply trying to survive. Through all the losses, all the chaos, their painful search was for safety, security, home. Today I still feel the poignancy of their longing for home.

The idea of home for bereaved Palestinians and Israelis weary of living in a fortress—rather than a home—is another complicated story of loss. In the West Bank, Lebanon, and Jordan where despair and anger boil over in desolate refugee camps, hatred for Israelis grows exponentially. Bitter stories about the systematic oppression and destruction of the Palestinian homeland and culture are rampant. Israelis, weary of intolerance and centuries-old discrimination, fight for a home of their own, fueling endless hostility and hatred. And if Palestinians cannot have a home, then Israelis will not have a home. Conversely, if Israel will not be a home, neither will Palestine. Israel has become a fortress and home for Palestinians exists only under the aegis of Israeli power. They are, all of them, refugees looking for home.

On U.S. borders, immigrants arrive every day seeking safety and asylum. Their yearning for a new beginning is etched into tired bodies and broken spirits, hollowed out places where survival has become their daily companion. Seeing their faces and hearing stories of innocent children—thousands of them—separated from parents and held in detention centers and refugee camps on American soil horrifies us. Another little known French artist has used street art to paint an oversized dining table straddling both sides of the U.S.-Mexico border at Tecate. A giant picnic table, he calls it—"people eating the same food, sharing the same water"—a place for all to be fed and welcomed.

What is it like to be a refugee fleeing unimaginable suffering and loss of identity, let alone a little child suddenly wrenched away from parents and family? How much desperation, how much fear does it take to leave the only home you know, a home you likely will never see again? When every door has closed, when daily life is unbearable, when one's very identity is shattered, there is no home. Will separated children placed in warehouses ever be able to survive and live a normal life? The notion of home seems impossibly remote. What, exactly, *is* home?

I visited Ellis Island a few months ago. Walking into the great hall where refugees from every corner of the world once huddled together, I found the names of my own ancestors who came through those same doors hoping to find home in America, looking for religious freedom, seeking a new future, longing for security and independence. Pictures of immigrants hang on every wall, their thin bodies and hollowed out eyes reminding all of us how little time has passed since our own forebears were refugees seeking home and a better life. They too came seeking freedom from oppression, hope for a new future, security. Today the statue that proclaims liberty in the harbor of New York City reminds us of our nation's solemn promise to the lost, the needy, the rejected, and the exiled. The Statue of Liberty—also named the Mother of Exiles—proclaims welcome to the tired and poor, the huddled masses, all who yearn to breathe free.

All of us who inhabit our earth home share a common humanity. We have a moral imperative to show compassion and empathy, to bind up the wounded and to make a home for all who are hurting and fearful. Leaving home and finding home never have been easy and we, all of us, are called to make the journey more bearable. *I was hungry and you gave me food; I was thirsty and you gave me drink; I was a stranger and you took me in; I was in prison and you came to me.*

Home is where God dwells, where there is hope, where diversity and difference are celebrated and honored. When we embrace one another in humility, in love and mutuality, God is there. We *are* God's dwelling place. We *are* God's home and we are called to make a home for all. Gather us in, O God, the lost and the lonely. Gather us in and make us your own. How desperately we all need home!

REFLECTION

All of us who inhabit our earth home share a common humanity. We have a moral imperative to show compassion and empathy, to bind up the wounded and to make a home for all who are hurting and fearful.

- Take a moment to read Leviticus 19 about the exile; Matthew 25 about the stranger; 2 Corinthians 8 about abundance.

- Describe your own experiences of immigration or of working with refugees.

- Go to http://brunocatalano.com/ to view his sculptures of refugees. What do *you* see?

- Go to https://hypebeast.com/2017/10/mexico-us-border-giant-picnic-jr to view the giant table straddling the border town of Tecate, Mexico. What do the eyes say to you?

21

RUNAWAY BUNNY

ERHAPS IT WAS AFTER the umpteenth reading of the always delightful children's book by Margaret Wise Brown, *The Runaway Bunny* or perhaps it followed my own retelling of this classic about a little bunny who wanted to run away.[1] Whatever it was, Elliot—with sparks of light in his eyes and a hint of clandestine camaraderie in his bearing—confided to me one day, "Grandma, did you know Ingrid and I have tried to run away from home?" After hearing their stories and affirming the "danger" and the adventure, I began my own tale.

I had just turned 8 and needing to flex my own independence and stubborn spirit, I said to my mother, "*I am running away.*" I do not remember the circumstances. Were my little sisters objecting to their bossy big sister? Perhaps I'd used words unacceptable to my mother. Or my father had laid down the law about something over which I disagreed. Evidently I felt powerless and needed to punish them all with my absence. Oh how they'd mourn once I was gone!

1. Margaret Wise Brown, *The Runaway Bunny* (New York: Harper and Row, 1942).

Runaway Bunny

It was still winter in cold Minnesota and we lived near a busy intersection I thought ideal for an adventure. Its noisy menace of city traffic just might serve as a reminder to my parents and sisters how much they were going to miss me. So I packed a sandwich and put on mittens and coat in preparation for heading out into the cold, cruel world. I knew how to cross the traffic-clogged streets and eventually found shelter in the outside entrance to a small bookstore. I wasn't brave enough to go inside but in the protection of its front doors, I could stand out of the wind and enjoy my lunch—a block away from home.

Before leaving home to make that long trek, I do not remember my mother saying that if I ran away, she would run after me. I knew I was her little bunny and I did not need to be reminded. She may even have helped me make the sandwich and reminded me to wear a warm woolen hat and big boots. She was very kind.

The cold was not so kind and the shelter of the bookstore entrance soon grew too small, too cramped. The wind and snow swirled around me and I worried that my parents might get stuck in the snowbanks lining the street when they came to rescue me. The peanut butter had also made me very thirsty and I knew not to eat a handful of snow or lick the ice sickles hanging off the low roof above the bookstore's windows. What was I to do?

Meanwhile at home, my mother began making lunch, a delicious pot of warm soup. I thought I could smell it from my cold perch a block away and I could also imagine my sisters playing in their bedroom between the twin beds where they'd made a fort with warm blankets and fat pillows. I thought they might need me to help them pick things up before our mother called us to lunch. So very slowly, I walked to the busy intersection, shivering all the way. When the light turned green, I looked both ways to make sure no cars were coming and then crossed over to the promised land on the other side. *If you run away, said her mother, I will make a pot of soup for your return.*

Home is where I learned to know God's love. Home is where I knew that *if I became a fish in a trout stream to swim away from home, my father would become a fisherman and he would come fishing for me.* And when I was a teenager trying to find myself in the complicated world of adolescence, I told my parents to forget fishing for me. I'd decided to *become a rock high up on the mountain side.* To this, my mother replied that if I became a rock high in the mountains, she could easily become a mountain climber who would climb to where I was. I sighed in exasperation.

Leaving home years later to go away to university, I left my peanut butter sandwich and the trout stream and the mountain top behind me. Using the wings my parents had given me and the courage I'd garnered along the way, I discovered a new home with many rivers and high mountains in every direction. When I went home to my family on breaks, there was always a warm pot of soup waiting and my siblings and parents wanted to know where the rivers ran and what the mountain climbing was like.

I knew too that if the fishing and the mountain climbing were unsuccessful escapes from home, I could become a colorful flower in a lovely garden. But of course my mother reminded me that *she was a gardener who always would be able to find me.* And so I left the beautiful gardens of my youth to explore distant places always carrying my mother's presence and hearing my father's voice—there was baggage with both. But packed inside those mostly comforting bags were unconditional love, respect and acceptance, grace. I knew they would always find me no matter how far I traveled.

This is how I came to know a loving God. This is how I found home. Some years after being found in the garden, I decided *to become a bird and fly away from home.* This time my dear spouse said, "Oh no! If you do this, I'll have to *become a tree for you to come home to*" to which I might have responded, *"Okay then! I'll need to be a little sailboat so that I can sail away to distant places . . ."*—halfhearted words, said always in a moment of frustration as we slowly learned to sail together. *If you run away, I will run after you . . .*

All along the way, I have been won over and buoyed by boundless love. All along the way, I have found God waiting for me, for us—patiently, persistently. All along the way, I have known unconditional love in the embrace of my family and in the presence of the Holy One, always waiting in the shadows to surprise and welcome us all home.

REFLECTION

This is how I came to know a loving God. This is how I found home . . . All along the way, I have been won over and buoyed by boundless love. All along the way, I have found God waiting for me, for us . . .

- Find a copy of *The Runaway Bunny* and savor its message of the boundless love of God.
- Have you ever run away from home? What was it like?
- Where or when have you found God waiting for you?
- How do you describe home?

22

Searching for home: Ljdja, Nadja, Alexander

HE NEWSPAPER HEADLINES COMING from the Balkans during the last decade of the twentieth century are what I remember best—frightening words like ethnic cleansing, genocide, civil war, and crimes against humanity. Recognizing the names of the countries was not difficult but identifying their geographical settings on the Balkan Peninsula was more challenging: Montenegro, Croatia, Bosnia and Hercegovina, Serbia, Slovenia—the vulnerable Balkans, each defining the others in partial truths; each a complex mix of identities, languages, religions; each struggling to define nationhood and the meaning of home.

Known for centuries of unrest but most recently for fighting one another over autonomy and some semblance of independence, the Balkans continue to search for economic stability and political and social identity. Spending brief time in all five countries recently, I came away with an unsettling sense of confused rootlessness which I interpret as a longing for home. The beautiful Slavic, European, Turkish, Jewish, Muslim, Orthodox, Catholic people of the Balkans seem to be haunted by their past and confused about their future. Caught in a centuries-long vortex of conflict, finding home is the story each of them tells with poignant urgency and tentative hope.

For Ljdja, a forty-something resident of Dubrovnik who grew up in the old city during the last major war, enthusiasm about her culture and the stunningly beautiful architecture surrounding her family's apartment on old Dubrovnik's main street seems to come easily. She expounds about music wafting from the open windows of the music school and she carries listeners away with lyrical descriptions of Croatian culture and history. She is proud of her home, her heritage, the beauty of her land. Leading us through the narrow streets, Ljdja exclaims about Croatia's past until we reach a small auditorium that once served as a church.

There, she switches directions and begins telling her rapt listeners that her home, her Croatia, is one disaster, one accident away from collapse. Its fragile economic base is dependent on newly popular, perhaps fickle tourism, likely unsustainable and unpredictable. Ljdja describes the exit of young people who cannot find jobs and a "brain drain" that takes the brightest and best educated away from the home of their birth to more promising and hopeful futures elsewhere. She is afraid for her country, for her own daughters, for the years ahead without adequate salaries, pensions, and political structures to support its people. Ljdja tells us that her Croatia is no longer home. Her Croatia is dying.

In Sarajevo, we are introduced to Nadja, a child during the worst of times and now a steely strong young adult committed to forensic work as a means of identifying the victims of ethnic cleansing—and fiercely determined to create home in her broken land. When I ask her about the death of her father when she was six years old, she brushes it off saying, "Nearly everyone lost parents, grandparents, family members. It was normal." As she leads us through a city still pock-marked with evidence of bombing and points to the mountains surrounding it, she describes a massacre we cannot comprehend. Only when we see graphic photos mounted near a tunnel where people hid and see the anguish in

Nadja's face as she leads us into the tunnel do *we* begin to feel the magnitude of the suffering. Bosnia-Herzegovina seems to have borne the brunt of Serbian nationalism, hatred, and fear of difference. And because there still are disparate groups living within this geographical area, they appear unable to govern or to find a way forward. For Bosnians, Bosniaks, Herzegovinians, Bosnian Serbs, and other factions we are unable to understand, finding home seems impossible and making a nation is too complex and elusive for any recognizable unity or definable identity.

We meet Alexander in Serbian Belgrade. A university student studying engineering, his youthful exuberance is contagious as he describes his family's five-acre farm along the banks of the Danube River. The orchards and fields are home for Alexander, the place his grandparents reclaimed after communism and subsequent political upheaval in the former Yugoslavia. It's where his parents built a home, shared now by aunts and uncles and cousins. He's optimistic about harvesting fruit and vegetables for a nearby village market and confident that his family can do well. He isn't hopeful about finding work related to his university studies. None of Alexander's Serbian contemporaries expect to work in their chosen field—there simply are not enough jobs and choice is an unexpected privilege.

He is curious about the world and tells us of a one-time visit to Prague, "the most beautiful city ever" he says, the kind of place he hopes his city will become. Alexander doesn't seem to labor over the atrocities of the past—perhaps he's too young. He quickly characterizes the surrounding Balkan states as corrupt and not trustworthy *or* generous and kind but incapable of making their government work *or* lazy but rich. And yet in Alexander's very bearing we sense a poignant sense of longing, a search for identity, a tangible yearning for the home he hopes Serbia will become.

Ljdja, Nadja, and Alexander all seem to be searching for home. Their war-torn corners of the world are rocky places filled with uncertainty and insecurity. Like many of us, they are looking for reliable roots, national identity, hope, and peace. Each embodies diversity that characterizes many places in the world, diversity that too often pits us against one another.

In this twenty-first century, how shall we learn to live with difference and celebrate our common humanity? How will we honor differing ways of understanding God to accept cultures and peoples different from ourselves? Can we walk together to save our beautiful planet, our earth home? Can we work for the common good to live with less comfort and more compassion, guarding against domination and privileged power to strive for peace and justice? We all are God's people. We all are God's dwelling place. We are, all of us, walking roads in search of home.

REFLECTION

For Ljdja, Nadja, and Alexander, their war-torn corners of the world are rocky places filled with uncertainty and insecurity. Like many of us, they are looking for reliable roots, national identity, hope, and peace. Each embodies diversity that characterizes many places in the world, diversity that too often pits us against one another.

- Describe how the experiences of these three reflect a search for home.

- What are some tangible ways to learn to live with difference to celebrate our common humanity?

- How might we honor differing ways of understanding God?

- Discuss how care of our earth home might be a common goal offering us shared opportunities for mutuality, trust.

- What does working for the common good look like?

23

Searching for Sunday

 E WERE WRONG" proclaims a recent article posted by BaptistNews.com.[1] With heartfelt words and a plea for his church to acknowledge certain convictions that have proven to be damaging and/or blatantly untrue, the writer describes his denomination's views on race and the role of women, on absolute certainty and rigid notions of biblical interpretation, on sexuality and gender identity. He admonishes his church for being more concerned with covering up clergy misconduct and making assumptions about what it means to be pro-life, of being more interested in numbers and image rather than the spirit—the souls—of her people. Reading it, I immediately felt a sense of despair as yet another blow was dealt an already wounded and often marginalized church.

We know too painfully that the church is not immune from arrogant pride, exclusivity and racism, or using its power and religiosity to do damage. The church often has "been wrong." White

1 Mark Wingfield, "3 Words for the Church in 2019: 'We Were Wrong.'"

evangelical support for leaders bent on undermining democracy and supporting totalitarian regimes or turning a blind eye to misogyny or abuse or denying climate change all contribute to the lack of credibility and trust. There are many good reasons for abandoning organized religion and finding community—home— in other places. And yes, there are many reasons for the despair that nips at our heels. "We were wrong" is a hymn of sorrow and mourning.

So it is that I write about searching for Sunday, for finding home in Sabbath time. On the racetrack that describes much about everyday life, many of us long to experience an alternative way. How do we live generously and with abundance? How do we make a difference? Can we live fearlessly? How do we lose our little lives for the bigger life of the world? What does it mean to be transformed? And for Christians, how do we see through the eyes of Jesus and feel through the heart of Christ? Might finding home in Sabbath practices or in other traditions that speak to justice and the common good, generosity of spirit, and responding to the world with healing love be a universal longing, a way of *finding home*?

Sunday is called Sabbath in my tradition. For Christians, Sunday is a day for taking stock and finding one's bearings. In addition to the rituals of worship, Sunday means family and friends, meals and celebrations, all holy reminders of God's presence in everyday life. Sunday is also a weekly Easter, a resurrection day set apart for renewal and new life, gifts of a mysterious God who replenishes and restores tired spirits and broken bodies. Slowly and mercifully, the habits of Sunday become a spiritual home—a time and place set apart, resurrection time.

Sunday connects us to others. It's more than habit or family-inherited commitments or socio-economic clubs of like-minded people, more than misplaced or exaggerated political hopes. Yes to political obligations and responsibilities. Yes to communities of friends and families. Yes to all the ways we gather together to learn and challenge and work with one another. God knows this world—our earth home—requires the engagement of every last one of us.

In the places where I gather to worship, I am fed, challenged, humbled, and emboldened by words and actions, signs and symbols, music and liturgy—acts of grace and mercy and love. These things are weekly reminders about sharing bread, welcoming strangers, embracing the refugee, working for justice, making peace, acting politically—literally becoming bread for the world. They anchor me in something bigger than myself and remind me that God's desire for wholeness is both communal and personal.

There is plenty to lament in the church as it lurches and hiccups its way in the world. Reasons for discounting religious institutions are legion and the church must be held accountable when it fails to acknowledge its brokenness. But the church, the body of Christ, is a visible gathering of all God's people who gather to declare their deepest hunger and thirst, their inadequacies and brokenness together with their cries for the healing and wholeness of all creation.

Searching for Sunday is a way of *finding home.* In all its iterations, failings, and inconsistencies, the church's Sunday is where we put ourselves because our lives and the life of the world depend on it. It's not about remarkable architecture or "cool" music or programs for every day of the week. It's not about making connections, self-help, or doing the right thing. It's not about what my parents believed or the traditions of my ancestors.

At its best, the church reminds us who we are and who Christ is. Sunday calls us from despair and hopelessness. It invites us home, reminds us that we are God's home, and directs us to make home for all. It calls us to be light, hope and grace, healers and comforters, the very hands and face of the Christ we worship, the mysterious God who is our true home.

REFLECTION

Searching for Sunday is a way of *finding home.* In all its iterations, failings, and inconsistencies, the church's Sunday is where we put ourselves because our lives and the life of the world depend on it.

- What do you lament or find lacking in your practice of Sabbath, of Sunday?

- How might the failings of the church reflect our own failings, our own brokenness?

- What do you understand the primary calling of the church to be?

- How might you describe practicing Sabbath time as finding home?

24

Two homes:
ALBERTO AND BERTA

HEN HOME IS NO longer a place of safety, comfort, or opportunity, harsh decisions force their way into already harsh circumstances. When you are still young and strong and able to put aside the uncertainty of what lies ahead, when family and neighbors and whole communities are running for their lives, when every other road seems closed, when your very survival is at stake, you run. It's an old story.

Like so many others, Alberto ran from Oaxaca in Mexico. When Alberto fled, there were not so many deterrents for entering a new country and he was able to cross the border legally. Work was plentiful and he loved this new land where he could work hard and think about a future without dread and fear. On a visit back to Mexico he met Berta, a preschool teacher also from Oaxaca. After courtship and marriage, Alberto brought Berta to the United States where she studied, took whatever jobs she could find, and eventually earned legal residency, allowing her to live and work permanently in the new land.

Two Homes: Alberto and Berta

Alberto and Berta wanted nothing more than a home for themselves, a secure future for their life together. When their children were young, they moved to a one-room "granny flat" near a three-acre plot of land where they began growing flower and vegetable starts to sell in local markets. Alberto planted the seeds and cared for the tender seedlings, learning to take thousands of cuttings to propagate new plants. Berta would rise at 3am each morning to begin the daily watering routine—20,000 seedlings all hand-watered until they were strong enough to sell, and together, they'd cart the plants to market. It was a good life but they wanted something more for their three children.

Berta's and Alberto's tiny home was just next door to an American family who'd lived in this rich agricultural valley for many years. Both teachers, David and Suzanne became friends and then role models for their immigrant neighbors—"Look at Mr. David and Mrs. Suzanne all dressed up and going off to teach school . . . ," Berta and Alberto would say. "You must work very hard at school. You must graduate and you must go to university" became their mantra. Berta and Alberto wanted their children's lives to be different from their own. They wanted their children to know the security they believed education would provide, a way of life that would illustrate they were no longer immigrants but had found true home in this new land.

One day it happened that Mr. David and Mrs. Suzanne offered to rent their next door home to Berta and Alberto. The "granny flat" where the immigrant family had lived for more than fifteen years was bursting at the seams and David and Suzanne no longer needed their house. The nominal rent they asked was far below market value and David and Suzanne knew that Berta and Alberto would not always have money enough for rent. But David and Suzanne were also doing their version of planting seeds by making possible an affordable home for an immigrant family whose children by now were planning their own futures.

As first one child went off to university to earn a degree in early childhood education, they all watched with a sense of hope and satisfaction. Then Berta and Alberto's second child began studies focusing on marine biology—more dreams being realized. The third, a very bright young man, has begun his first year at university even as he works to overcome his love for video games. He too wants to concentrate on academics like his siblings have done. David and Suzanne watch each with obvious satisfaction. Berta's and Alberto's deep pride and pleasure is palpable.

Two homes then—a one-room flat where an immigrant family dreamed about a better life for their children and a home next door where the benefits of education gave visible expression to that better way of life. Friendship and mutuality enriched both homes; trust and compassion were obvious components. These two homes embody the best of humanity: a family working hard to insure that their children will become contributing members in their new land, and another successful family willing to believe they too can make a difference, that they too have obligations.

Both families are planters of seeds, both know the significance of home; both find fulfillment and joy in being part of something bigger than themselves. David and Suzanne say this is not a unique story, that this kind of generosity and grace is commonplace and happens over and over again. I am a grateful recipient of their story, pleased to tell it, and glad for the many ways it affirms our common humanity and our common responsibility. Finding home indeed!

REFLECTION

Two homes then—a one-room flat where an immigrant family dreamed about a better life for their children and a home next door where the benefits of education gave visible expression to that better way of life.

- Do stories like this matter? Why or why not?
- How does this story transcend ethnic, cultural, and religious differences?
- Describe some multiple meanings about how this story illustrates the common humanity of "finding home."

25

Two cabins

FOR THE LONGEST TIME the cabin was just one big room. When we got tired of running between the apple trees to a shingled outhouse near the hill behind the cabin, our father patched together a bathroom in one corner. To his credit, this tiny room did have a window and our pleasure over being able finally to take summer showers may have been greater than the pleasure of no longer making night runs to the old outhouse. That small corner gave the cabin a second room, the kitchen space now sharing its western views with the indoor bathroom and the rest of the large room serving as bedroom, living room, and dining room. When a new floor was laid about the same time as the debut of the bathroom, we wrote notes and laid them on the bare wood beneath the new linoleum—to be found decades later.

We loved this cabin on the island built with hand-hewn fir logs by my grandparents and their sons. None of them were perfectionists but it was a solid achievement, this cabin whose rough log walls needed regular coats of linseed oil to protect them from insects. Scratchy oakum was used to chink the spaces between each log and a beautiful tongue and groove cedar ceiling together with the fragrant logs gave off a distinctive smell I will remember until the day I die.

My mother made our summer getaway situated at the edge of the shoreline a home. Her pleasure over turning an old spice cabinet into a cupboard or finding brightly colored oil cloth to cover the big oval table or inviting extended family to come for a Sunday picnic shaped much of my sense of home. But no one loved the cabin like my father. Its place on North Beach in a spectacularly beautiful chain of islands called the San Juans anchored him to his childhood and reminded him of rowing with his mother from one island to another. Boats and tides and weather were his passions and the cabin their stage.

The essence of what our cabin home conveyed to me as a child is the security of belonging. Surrounded there by parents and siblings, grandparents, aunts, uncles, and cousins, we learned who we were, what we valued, and what God might be like. Family stories and myths bigger than life were the currency of every gathering. And around tables laden with seafood and the recipes of a family who loved to cook, I took away resilience and self-reliance together with a keen sense of the attributes that make finding home so formative.

Many years later, a second cabin began claiming its place of prominence as a backdrop for understanding the significance of home. Like the island cabin, its iconic physical and geographical setting is interwoven in family stories and traditions. On the western front of the Rocky Mountains alongside a stunningly beautiful national park, this cabin became a siren call luring us from our home in the Midwest for summer breaks and winter getaways. From the beginning, it too was graced by grandparents and extended family planting it deep in the psyches of my own children. When they were old enough to be able to spend summers working in the park, the cabin—now named Red Vest—became a hub for friends and roommates and friends of friends. Later on, each of our daughters' weddings took place there, together with family gatherings and a steady stream of summer visitors who continue to fill that high-ceilinged, many-roomed house with unforgettable memories.

How does one measure the meanings of home? At Red Vest, the early morning play of grandchildren whose own sense of home is being shaped and formed is one way. My spouse's library above the garage where he works and finds so much pleasure in this season of our lives is another. The time we spend together during the long days of summer is treasured and a reminder that life is short and we have only so much time to make it worthwhile. The fact that our daughters and sons-in-laws continue to come—often overlapping their visits in order to hike and camp and spend time together—means that every bed is filled, every corner occupied. Our table too is laden with good food and the cabin's pantry well-stocked. The days when we no longer have the energy or ability to keep this all going will arrive soon enough. For now, we make the most of this cabin home knowing it as a treasured gift to be shared.

Perhaps that's the true measure of the meaning of home—the ways in which we share our lives and ourselves, sometimes broken and dysfunctional, occasionally joy-filled, often mundane and ordinary—in places that provide safety and shelter and security, true hospitality. Home *is* where we learn who we are and what the world is like. It also must be where we learn compassion and responsibility for those who have no home, no safe place. May our doors be always open. May we make generous space for welcome and acceptance. In the words of poet Henri-Frederic Amiel, "Life is short and we do not have much time to gladden the hearts of those who travel the way with us. So be swift to love. Make haste to be kind. And go in peace to love and serve God." In so doing, we find home.

REFLECTION

The essence of what "the cabin" conveyed to me as a child and later as an adult is the security of belonging and the joy of shared life; . . . perhaps that's the true measure of the meaning of home.

- What are some characteristics of the places that feel most like home to you?

- How would you describe hospitality or what it might mean to share home?

- Home always is fraught with complexity. If you have not felt home to be a place of belonging, where else have you found acceptance and welcome?

- Reread the quote from poet, Henri-Frederic Amiel. How does it get at the essence of home?

26

We were at home there

O MANY IMAGES SWIM just below the surface of my memory, all the houses where I came to know home. It takes little to retrieve them: "Remember when Grandma told us she was ready to die? She was sitting right there by the fireplace and I didn't want to hear it!" or "Do you remember the time—just after the snow finally had melted—that we convinced Dad we needed a trampoline?" or "This is where Grandpa helped me make a kite from old newspapers. We flew it above the beach where the wind could catch it. I'd have liked more time to get to know him and I have so many questions I'd like answered"—stories told for decades in the varied iterations of the various tellers ... "Do you remember?"

There are smells like the acrid pungency of saltwater tide flats on the island where I grew up or the scent of wafting smoke from coal fires on a drizzly winter day in England or the sound of rain on a tin roof or the whishing gasps of a braking bus. All evoke times and places imprinted in my psyche. Sure triggers are memories of births and birthdays, of holy days and holidays, of arrivals and departures—flashing through one's mind like a slow-motion movie filled with familiar faces and poignant reminders of time and place, houses and home.

They came in all shapes and sizes: a tiny box of house set in a small mountain town where I learned the Nativity story; a narrow house made of corrugated steel and named "the tin house" by my young sisters and me; my grandparents' homes, the one built on a mound of rock overlooking the channel where ships and ferries crisscrossed day after day and the other, a large, white-sided arts-and-crafts home surrounded by fruit trees and well-tended gardens. This one appears often in my dreams and became the family gathering place with its seemingly endless spaces for hiding and playing and discovering family stories. We were at home there.

There are apartments and flats where we learned to live in close proximity with others, an island cabin made of hand-hewn logs and a mountain house near a river, both of these iconic in their larger-than-life roles. In Minnesota, we found our dream house during my daughters' growing up years—an elegant English Tudor where we hosted sleep-overs and faculty gatherings and students from around the world. We were at home there too.

Make no mistake: none of these homes were perfect and every one of them has known its share of dysfunction. But from my childhood until now, these are places where I've encountered grace and unconditional love, shelter and security. In all their convoluted complexity, these are the places where I've learned family history, religious identity, and resilient faith. In the island cabin made of logs, we discovered the natural world in the cyclical coming and going of tides and in the change of seasons. The mountain house has been graced with the passing of generations, the weddings of daughters, transitions, and a steady stream of family and friends who come to enjoy its embrace and surrounding beauty.

There are stories of brokenness and sorrow, betrayals and disappointments. I do not forget them and the anguish they still elicit. But stronger still are the moments of joy when we connected with one another, discovering each other's idiosyncrasies and quirky characteristics, learning to make the passages from one stage of life to another, sharing the pleasure of belonging to our particular tribes.

In an old classic, *The House by the Dvina,* author Eugenie Fraser tells a compelling story of her ancestors before, during, and after the Russian Revolution that began in 1917.[1] Grounded in a mythic family home along the Dvina River in Archangel, Fraser vividly describes the times and places where she came to know herself and her people, their joys and sorrows, traditions and customs. She too would say, "Despite all the losses, we were at home there."

In another archetypal tale of home, *The Septembers of Shiraz* by Dalia Sofer,[2] its main character, Parviz has been sent to New York by his family hoping he might escape the dystopian life of revolutionary Iran. Now living alone in Brooklyn and desperately lonesome for his Persian home, Parviz observes the students in his architecture class imagining them growing up in the clean-lined, sunny American homes projected on the classroom's overhead screen. His observation is another poignant reminder that this is not his home and that these classmates are products of a land and place where he may never be able to say, "I was at home there."

Each of the homes I describe implies the trust, safety, and peace that come from having a place where in one way or another, one *belongs.* These homes may be literal and metaphorical, physical and emotional, spiritual, imagined—the actual homes of my grandparents, our lovely old Minnesota house, a way of life longed for by millions of refugees, the many meanings of shelter, our work, our bodies, our religious and political identities.

Writer and teacher, Diana Butler Bass speaks of home as *grounding,* literally the places where our feet touch the ground and where we know in our bones that we are home. Another writer, Jan Richardson, has written a lovely blessing containing the beauty of home called "The Year as a House." Poet Mary Oliver says of our earth home, "My work is loving the world, which is mostly

---

1. Eugenie Fraser, *The House by the Dvina: A Russian Childhood* (London: Corgi, 1984).

2. Dalia Sofer, *The Septembers of Shiraz* (New York: Ecco, 2007).

standing still and learning to be astonished." Or in the words of
Frederick Buechner, home is the manger in Bethlehem, the place
where at midnight, even the oxen kneel. In all these interpretations
and iterations, I want to be able to say "we were at home there."
Finding home defines our identity. Finding home is a radical act of
claiming our place in the world.

REFLECTION

So many images swim just below the surface of my memory, all
the houses where I came to know home. It takes little to retrieve
them. . . . Whether literal or metaphorical, each implies the trust,
safety, and peace that come from having a place where in one way
or another, one *belongs*.

- Home means so many things. How might you describe finding home for yourself?
- Home is never a static thing. How has your sense of home
  changed over time?
- Describe some places where despite all the complexities you
  can say, "We were at home there."
- Why is finding home so important for all of us?

Epilogue

NE WEEK AFTER SUBMITTING the manuscript for *Finding Home* to my publisher, the world shifted dramatically. Rumors and still distant reports from central China about a deadly virus suddenly struck close to home. The first person to be diagnosed in our state was a man who worked in the elementary school where our grandson is a first-grader. As the community went into high alert and our own family self-quarantined, the coronavirus suddenly became an alarming reality we could no longer hold at arm's length. No more visits between our homes. No more watching China and Italy and France from a safe distance. No more living each day of our comfortable lives as if we are somehow protected from devastation and the ravages wreaking havoc around the globe. If ever we'd had a sense of home as invulnerable or invincible or at the very least, a secure place of protection, that too was shattered.

As I write today, millions are locked down in their homes hoping to protect themselves and their neighbors from the spread of COVID-19, the coronavirus that has become a household word. This afternoon I will visit via phone with a dear friend in the United Kingdom who yesterday marked the death of a family member whose dying will not be honored with a funeral since no one could attend. Haunting images of thousands of caskets lined up in the churches of Northern Italy waiting for burial make our hearts ache with sorrow. Hundreds more are stacked on trucks and wagons lining roads to cemeteries where there is no more room for so many bodies.

All of us wake in the morning to reports of a global disaster few could have imagined and if we've managed the task of going to sleep at night, it's with never-ending images and voices coming at us like arrows in a science-fiction movie. Sickness and death seem to lurk in every community and we're told again and again that social isolation is the only hope of slowing its exponential growth. Fearing the worst, our homes have become fortresses in which we all hide to seek protection. In country after country and state after state, laws have been enacted requiring citizens to shelter at home. Ordinary daily life has come to a grinding halt as we seek to find home as a protective shelter.

Without a doubt, our current crisis will continue to unfold, changing life in ways we cannot yet see or predict or even prepare for. What may be clearest to us in this perilous moment is our interconnectedness, the fact that we share a common home with all of humanity. Our inextricable links to one another have never been more graphic. In a period of history inclined toward extreme nationalism and heightened individualism, a global pandemic may help us reclaim and redefine mutuality and interdependence. Perhaps a seismic epidemic will strip us of our penchant for exceptionalism and remind us of shared humanity and our place in the panoply of humankind. Hopefully, we will begin to see this frail planet as our common home and disease as a common enemy uniting the human family rather than setting us against one another.

As I wait for the publication of *Finding Home*, I have a dream that this latest catastrophe will become an opportunity for showing us a new way of being. The virulent virus threatening our globe is said to have come from live bats sold in the wet markets of central China. I walked in similar wet markets along the Mekong Delta in Southeast Asia only a few months ago—a foreign place where I learned to feel at home. I have a dream that our current crisis will unite us with neighbors around the world, sharing research and scientific data to help eradicate deadly diseases. I have a dream that we will recognize again our need for each other, creating alliances and organizations to protect the whole of humanity. I have a dream that we will no longer call for walls of separation to divide and keep others out and instead build bridges of understanding that foster justice, peace, and safety for all. I have a dream that we will unite to help save our uniquely beautiful planet from abuse and greed and global destruction. And I have a dream that in our common longing for home as a place for finding shelter and safety, we truly will learn what it means to be home for each other. In the coming days, there may be no more important task before us than relearning what it means to belong to one another, to share a common home, to think communally and globally, for the common good and for the sake of the world.

Julie K. Aageson

Resources

Aageson, Julie K. *Benedictions: 26 Reflections*. Eugene, OR: Wipf and Stock, 2016.

——. *Holy Ground: An Alphabet of Prayer*. Eugene, OR: Cascade, 2018.

Bass, Diana Butler. *Grounded: Finding God in the World—A Spiritual Revolution*. New York: HarperOne, 2015.

Bondi, Roberta C. *Houses: A Family Memoir of Grace*. Nashville: Abingdon, 2000.

Bonhoeffer, Dietrich. *Letters and Papers from Prison*. New York: Macmillan, 1971.

Brocker, Mark. *Coming Home to Earth*. Eugene, OR: Cascade, 2016.

Brown, Margaret Wise. *The Runaway Bunny*. New York: Harper and Row, 1942.

Evangelical Lutheran Worship. Minneapolis: Augsburg Fortress, 2006.

Fraser, Eugenie. *The House by the Dvina: A Russian Childhood*. London: Corgi, 1984.

Ingraham, Christopher. *If You Lived Here You'd Be Home by Now*. New York: Harper, 2019.

Molton, Warren L. "If God Is Your Answer." *Christian Century*, June 14, 2004. https://www.christiancentury.org/artsculture/poems/if-god-your-answer

Norris, Gunilla. *Being Home: Discovering the Spiritual in the Everyday*. Mahwah, NJ: Hidden Spring, 2001.

O'Tuama, Padraig. *In the Shelter: Finding a Home in the World*. London: Hodder and Stoughton, 2015.

Robinson, Marilynne. *Gilead*. New York: Picador, 2004.

——. *Housekeeping*. New York: Picador, 1980.

——. *Lila*. New York: Picador, 2014.

Rybczynski, Witold. *Home: A Short History of an Idea*. New York: Penguin, 1986.

Sofer, Dalia. *The Septembers of Shiraz*. New York: Ecco, 2007.

Taylor, Barbara Brown. *Learning to Walk in the Dark*. New York: HarperOne, 2014.

Thich Nhat Hanh. *Gathas of Thich Nhat Hanh*. Online at https://beherenownetwork.com/thich-nhat-hanh-gathas.

Resources

Wingfield, Mark. "3 Words for the Church in 2019: 'We Were Wrong.'" *Baptist News Global.* January 1, 2019. https://baptistnews.com/article/3-words-for-the-church-in-2019-we-were-wrong/#.XtZRMZ7Yqfc.